Contemporary Issues in Globalization

To my parents

Contemporary Issues in Globalization

An Introduction to Theory and
Policy in India

SOUMYEN SIKDAR

OXFORD
UNIVERSITY PRESS

OXFORD
UNIVERSITY PRESS

YMCA Library Building, Jai Singh Road, New Delhi 110001

Oxford University Press is a department of the University of Oxford. It
furthers the University's objective of excellence in research, scholarship, and
education by publishing worldwide in

Oxford   New York

Auckland   Bangkok   Buenos Aires   Cape Town   Chennai
Dar es Salaam   Delhi   Hong Kong   Istanbul   Karachi   Kolkata
Kuala Lumpur   Madrid   Melbourne   Mexico City   Mumbai   Nairobi
São Paulo   Shanghai Taipei   Tokyo   Toronto

Oxford is a registered trade mark of Oxford University Press
in the UK and in certain other countries

Published in India
By Oxford University Press, New Delhi

ISBN   019 5671120

Typeset in Adobe Garamond 10.5 on 12
By Jojy Philip, New Delhi 110027
Printed at Roopak Printers, New Delhi 110032
Published by Manzar Khan, Oxford University Press
YMCA Library Building, Jai Singh Road, New Delhi 110 001

Foreword

I have great pleasure in writing a foreword to this volume by Soumyen Sikdar on the theory and policy of liberalization and globalization in India.

My association of more than thirty years with the author has been a uniformly pleasant one. As a very bright undergraduate in our Economics Honours classes he impressed his teachers by his easy mastery of the arguments presented; what was even more impressive is that the questions that he asked would often go beyond the limits of the courses; questions that made the teacher try to rework the arguments. I am not at all certain how much credit I can claim for introducing economics to good students, but I have certainly learnt a lot myself in trying to meet their queries and objections. And in this respect I owe Soumyen a substantial debt for our exchanges over the years. I have been fortunate in knowing him as a student, a colleague, and later, a friend who always kept in touch. Soumyen keeps on plying me with books he likes. Only a fraction belongs to economics. Post structural theory, Turing machines or the Voyage of the Beagle, or even more recherché areas provoke his interest. Then I have to read these books and we talk about them. The breadth of his interests can be seen from the fact that his first monograph was a brief introduction to the history of Russian literature in Bengali.

Coming to his current monograph, it is not only for the advanced student of economics. Many others should find it profitable to get a clear view of the issues. Liberalization and globalization are words which provoke very sharp reactions—war cries for some, dirty thirteen or fourteen letter words for others. If someone were to try to make up ones own mind in these matters, both sides of the debate should first be discussed as dispassionately as possible. Sikdar meets this need, in my opinion, very successfully.

The case for economic liberalization has a hallowed tradition in which Adam Smith is the most important name. Similarly, the case for external liberalization was founded on David Ricardo's arguments. There was, of course, no general acceptance of the policy of liberalization, internal and external, by governments, and the German economist, Friedrich List, contested the British economists on theoretical grounds. So what is new about this debate?

Sikdar points out that the pace of technical innovation is incomparably fast today relative to say 1850–1950 AD; and that information technology (IT) has evolved to a stage where the producer just sits in his office and controls the flow of inputs from all over the world. But this office can be virtually anywhere. Add to this a very high rate of economic obsolescence of production processes and we get shorter recovery periods for investment, and so the search for larger and larger markets is on.

A straightforward 'no' to liberalization and globalization is out of the question. Who wants to go primitive? Certainly not the poor. If we want access to the advances in technology we have to let in large multinationals with the power to invest or disinvest whenever .

If we can't beat them then let us join them; why oppose them at all? The answer has several prongs: (1) The simple case for liberalization rests on several assumptions, for example, no monopolies, no externalities. Large multinationals appear to have scant regard for other people's environment. A minimalist government would not do; a very active public policy of regulation in respect of environmental damage (and of other externalities) is required. (2) External liberalization or globalization would do away with barriers to free movement of goods, equipment, inputs, and finance capital. It would also mean floating exchange rates and portfolio investment in our financial markets. Such systems exhibit a degree of volatility which might lead to economic disaster even when the basics are right. (3) High-tech means low employment potential. The distribution of income could worsen sharply enough to destabilize the system. Under plausible assumptions rich countries get richer while the globalized poor countries get (relatively) poorer.

It would not do, therefore, to let in hosts of multinationals who prowl around and strain and strive for larger shares of the liberalized world economy. No country, in fact, permits total liberalization. How do other countries cope? Sikdar discusses all the major strategies adopted by several countries.

The reader who perseveres should find it very enlightening. If one were to seek information about specific items, for example, intellectual property rights, they are all laid out clearly. I have learnt a lot from reading the book and I have enjoyed reading it because it is so clearly written—hardly any algebra to scare off the non-specialist, but several diagrams to help understand. Complex issues seldom have simple solutions; also economics can take one only so far. Social, historical, and political forces often make the economist come a cropper regarding the consequences of any act of policy. Sikdar writes here as a committed agnostic: he does not believe in faith but relies on straight thinking to take us some way towards understanding the world.

He deserves a wide readership both for content and style.

DIPAK BANERJEE[1]

---

[1] Formerly, Professor of Economics, Presidency College, Kolkata.

Acknowledgments

I am indebted to my friend Anindya Sen of the Indian Institute of Management (Kolkata), who made helpful suggestions and provided access to the valuable resources of the library of his institute. He was also instrumental in putting me in contact with the Oxford University Press. One can hardly hope for a better publishing house. Thanks are due to the students of Economics Honours at the Presidency College, to those of the Calcutta University at the master's level, and to the participants of seminars and refresher courses for college teachers organized by the universities of Calcutta, Burdwan, and Kalyani. Stimulating interaction with these diverse but extremely lively groups first made me feel the lack of a readily available text that covered with reasonable rigour and manageable detail the complex issues surrounding liberalization and globalization. Dipak Banerjee could not refuse an old student and kindly consented to contribute a foreword. I am grateful to him. Finally, I cannot adequately thank my wife, Paramita, who provided critical emotional and intellectual support during the period this book was written.

SOUMYEN SIKDAR

Contents

Tables

Figures

Boxes

Abbreviations

ACM	Arab Common Market
AFTA	Asian Free Trade Area
AMS	Aggregate Measure of Support
ANCOM	Andean Common Market
ANZCERTA	Australia–New Zealand Closer Economic Relations Trade Agreement
APEC	Asia Pacific Economic Cooperation Forum
ASEAN	Association of South East Asian Nations
BALCO	Bharat Aluminium Company
BoP	Balance of Payments
BoT	Balance of Trade
BOT	Build Operate Transfer
BT	British Telecom
CAB	Current Account Balance
CAP	Common Agricultural Policy
CARICOM	Caribbean Community
CBD	Convention on Biological Diversity
CEFTA	Central European Free Trade Area
CFC	chlorofluorocarbons
CPIAL	Consumer Price Index for Agricultural Labour
CPR	Common Property Resources
CU	Customs Union
DC	Developed Country

DFI	Direct Foreign Investment
DoT	Department of Telecommunications
DPCO	Drug Price Control Order
DSB	Dispute Settlement Body
ECPR	Efficient Component Pricing Rule
EEC	European Economic Community
EFTA	European Free Trade Association
EMS	European Monetary System
EPZ	Export Processing Zones
ERM	Exchange Rate Mechanism
ERP	Effective Rate of Protection
EU	European Union
FCCC	Framework Convention on Climate Change
FTA	Free Trade Area
FTZ	Free Trade Zones
GATS	General Agreement on Trade in Services
GATT	General Agreement on Tariffs and Trade
GCC	Gulf Cooperation Council
GDP	Gross Domestic Product
GNP	Gross National Product
GSP	Generalized System of Preference
IBRD	International Bank for Reconstruction and Development
IGIDR	Indira Gandhi Institute of Development Research
ILO	International Labour Organization
IMF	International Monetary Fund
IPR	Intellectual Property Rights
ISEW	Index of Sustainable Economic Welfare
ISO	International Standards Organization
IT	Information Technology
JNR	Japan National Railways
JT	Japan Tobacco
LBO	Leveraged Buyout

LDC	Less Developed Country
LIBOR	London Interbank Offered Rate
LIFFE	London International Financial Futures Exchange
LTA	Long Term Arrangement
M&A	Mergers & Acquisitions
MAI	Multilateral Agreement on Investment
MBO	Management Buyout
MEA	multilateral environment agreements
MERCOSUR	Southern Cone Common Market
MFA	Multifibre Arrangement
MFN	Most Favoured Nation
MITI	Ministry of International Trade and Industry
MNC	Multinational Corporations
MRTP	Monopolies and Restrictive Trade Practices Act
MRTS	Mass Rapid Transport System
MTNL	Mahanagar Telephone Nigam Limited
NAAEC	North American Agreement on Environmental Cooperation
NAFTA	North American Free Trade Agreement
NIC	Newly Industrializing Countries
NTB	Non-Tariff Barriers
NTT	Nippon Telegraph and Telephone
NRI	Non-Resident Indians
NRP	Nominal Rate of Protection
OECD	Organization for Economic Cooperation and Development
OPEC	Organization of Petroleum Exporting Countries
OTC	over the counter
PCB	Pollution Control Board
PFI	Portfolio Foreign Investment
PSBR	Public Sector Borrowing Requirement
PSE	Public Sector Enterprise
RBI	Reserve Bank of India

R&D	Research & Development
RER	Real Exchange Rate
RPI	Retail Price Index
RTB	Regional Trading Blocs
SDR	Special Drawing Right
SEBI	Securities and Exchange Board of India
SIMEX	Singapore International Monetary Exchange
SPM	Suspended particulate matter
SWIFT	Society for Worldwide Interbank Financial Telecommunication
TFP	Total Factor Productivity
TRAI	Telecommunications Regulatory Authority of India
TRIMS	Trade Related Investment Measures
TRIPS	Trade Related Intellectual Property Rights
UNCTAD	United Nation's Conference on Trade and Development
UNDP	United Nations Development Programme
UNEP	United Nation's Environment Programme
UPOV	Union for the Protection of Plant Varieties
VER	voluntary export restraints
VSNL	Videsh Sanchar Nigam Limited
WEO	World Environmental Organization
WHO	World Health Organization
WIPO	World Intellectual Property Organization
WTO	World Trade Organization
WTP	willingness to pay

ONE

Introduction

> The world has narrowed to a neighbourhood before it has
> broadened into a brotherhood.
>
> Lyndon B. Johnson

An almost obsessive preoccupation with 'liberal' and 'global' seems to have gripped the world since the end of the cold war. This has been accompanied by the ascendancy of the neoliberal ideology, also known informally as the Washington Consensus, that points emphatically in the direction of freer markets and reduced states. Everybody at large, politician, policy-maker, policy analyst, or journalist, is waving the banner of a new world order and spouting its rhetoric. Singapore's Deputy Prime Minister Lee Hsien Loong aptly summarized the widespread sentiment in a speech to policy-makers in Washington, DC in May 1998:

Globalization fostered by free flow of information and rapid progress in technology is a driving force that no country can turn back. It does impose market discipline on the participants, which can be harsh, but is the mechanism that drives progress and prosperity.

Setting rhetoric aside, let us take a closer look at the twin phenomena of liberalization and globalization to gain a better understanding of their nature and consequences. They are very much interlinked, as will become clear from this discussion.

Liberalization and globalization are both part of the programme of economic reform undertaken by dozens of countries in the last decade to give a new shape and direction to their economies. This programme represents a most radical departure from the theory and practice of development planning that had such a powerful grip on policy-makers in the backward economies of Asia, Africa, and Latin America in the post-war years.

Liberalization is the diminution or progressive elimination of the control of the state over economic activities. It is driven by the neoliberal idea that government involvement should be as low as possible (minimalist state), leaving the field to the operation of self-interest driven market forces of demand and supply. By stifling private initiative, persistent state control tends to bring about and perpetuate a situation of inefficiency and stagnation. Unshackling of the forces of competition is expected to reverse this and relaunch the system on a dynamic path to prosperity.

A programme of liberalization in this sense can have two dimensions, internal and external. Purely internal reform confines its attention to the domestic economy and takes measures to make it more responsive to market forces. Private agents are granted freedom to make their own decisions regarding consumption, production, input choice, pricing, marketing, lending, and borrowing and investment, both long term and short term, within the national economy. Full control, however, is retained over activities relating to the interface with the rest of the world (the external sector).

External liberalization, on the other hand, consists of relaxation of state control in the spheres of foreign trade, foreign investment, and flow of finance in and out of the country. The major components are— elimination of import duties and quantitative restrictions on trade, abolition of multiple exchange rates for the currency, devaluation of the unified rate, and restoration of full convertibility on current and capital accounts of the balance of payments (BoPs). The primary objective is to reap the potential benefits from greater participation in the resource flows of the world economy at large. External liberalization in this sense is alternatively known as adoption of a policy of globalization by the country concerned. Thus when a country wants to globalize it is undertaking a particular form of liberalization.

Globalization or external liberalization as a deliberately adopted economic policy is intimately connected with the phenomenon of globalization as a process that has been sweeping the world over the last couple of decades. This is an ongoing process of international integration as a result of unprecedented acceleration in the flow of trade, assets, technology, knowledge, information, and ideas (not to forget guns, drugs, and diseases) across national boundaries. It implies that domestic policies have prompt international repercussions and as a result national governments are much more constrained than they used to be in policy formulation and implementation.

Rising share of foreign trade in the activities of nations has naturally been a major feature of enhanced integration. Over the last forty years, a six-fold rise in world gross national product (GNP) has been accompanied by a twelve-fold increase in world trade. For the industrial countries the proportion of exports in gross domestic product (GDP) increased from 12 per cent in 1973 to 18 per cent in 1992. As a proportion of the total production of commodities the importance of trade is much larger, since the share of services (including government services) in GDP has increased dramatically over this period and most of these were not tradable.

Expanding international trade is just one of many manifestations of growing economic integration. Others are mobility of factors of production and exchange of assets. The global transaction of foreign exchange has reached incredible levels. From an average of US$ 15 billion a day in 1973 it grew to an average of US$ 1260 billion a day in 1995, seventy times the value of world trade per day! (This harbours great potential for disaster, as shall be seen later.)

If called upon to identify the principal factors that set the spiral of globalization moving and keep it moving, an economist is likely to come up with the following:

1. Increasing pace of technological innovation has dramatically shortened the economic life cycle of processes and products. Rapid obsolescence implies that the investments in research and expensive machinery have to be recovered in shorter and shorter periods. This necessitates continuous discovery of sales outlets. Globalization is an insatiable and restless search for markets by giant multinationals spread over ever expanding sections of the globe.

2. The IT revolution that has swept through the world in the last decade has radically transformed production processes and made the management of production facilities scattered over several countries much easier. Rapid advance in communication technology contributed to the creation of global markets through quick transmission of spectacular images of the lifestyle of western consumers to every corner of the world.

3. Advancing production technology and easier communication have enabled multinational corporations (MNCs) to finetune the value chain. Parts and components are routinely sourced from different countries and intrafirm trade among affiliates and subsidiaries of the multinationals accounts for a substantial portion of global trade.

The result is deep integration through an intricate networking of production, assembly, and marketing. For example, in designing advanced elevator systems, OTIS finds it normal to get motor drives from Japan, door systems from France, electronics from Germany, and small gear components from Spain. It was once calculated that the components of one 15 gram cup of strawberry yoghurt travelled more than one thousand kilometers—strawberries from Poland, corn and wheatflour from Holland, jam from West Germany, sugarbeet from East Germany, aluminium foil from Italy, and container cup from Malaysia! And the product is consumed in Addis Ababa, Beijing, Delhi, London, Sydney, and Lima.

4. It is not an exaggeration to say that the IT revolution was responsible in a big way for the collapse of socialism. Fed on lies about the west, the citizens of the erstwhile communist countries could no longer be kept perpetually in ignorance and deprivation. The collapse left the field unchallenged for capitalism by delivering a crushing blow to the Soviet model of planned economic development (centralized planning from above). Widespread dissatisfaction with the model had been growing anyway for quite some time before the actual crash. One after another, the countries in the third world attempted to move out of planning and regulation and build market-friendly, outward-oriented economic structures. Their governments started tumbling over each other to entice foreign capital in order to create employment and to gain access to modern technology and marketing skills. They wanted desperately to join the mainstream of global trade and investment so as not to be left behind any more. This change of policy was not always a result of free choice. In addition to the hope of benefiting from global links, it was also a response to heavy pressures exerted by the World Bank and the International Monetary Fund (IMF), who insisted on liberalization and export orientation as part of the conditionalities for the grant of assistance for stabilization and structural adjustment. India was no exception, but its overall approach towards both liberalization (internal) and global-ization has been rather cautious and slow

JUSTIFICATION OF LIBERALIZATION AND GLOBALIZATION

The best justification for globalization was provided long ago by John Stuart Mill:

It is hardly possible to overrate the value in the present low state of human improvement of placing human beings in contact with persons dissimilar to themselves, and with modes of thought and action unlike those with which they are familiar. Such communication has always been, peculiarly in the present age, one of the primary sources of progress.

The case for liberalization was created by the state of stagnation in which the planned economies languished after decades of pervasive state intervention. Massive misallocation of resources, low productivity all around, alarming growth in bureaucracy, inefficiency, and corruption, and persistence of severe poverty and income inequality often accompanied by political repression ultimately made a radical reorientation of policy unavoidable. Realizing the gravity of the situation, China started her programme in 1979. India's programme was initiated only in 1991. In Russia Mikhail Gorbachev's attempt failed, as it came too late and the problem by then had gone completely out of control.

A second argument for globalization is that isolation is no longer an option for India, given that other low income countries such as China, Indonesia, Sri Lanka, Thailand, Turkey, and Malaysia have decided to embrace it as policy. Our competitive position relative to these countries is already fairly weak. A further widening of the gap will wipe us off the economic map of the world. It is now a matter of survival in a fiercely competitive world. Accepting global integration as a fact, the urgent task ahead is to make the best use of the opportunities opened up. The task will not be easy, but the situation will have to be squarely faced.

THE DANGERS

Three major potential dangers for a country may be identified.

Increased Exposure to Risk

A country that is deeply involved in the international network of production and investment exposes itself to the unpredictable ups and downs of global business and to the policy mistakes of other countries. Diversification is the way to reduce risk, but reliance on exports requires specialization in a small number of activities, which is a movement away from diversification. A sharp fall in the price of exportables in the world market will cause a steep decline in national income with associated loss of employment. Although unskilled or semi-skilled labour is usually the first casualty of recession, even skilled labour is by no means immune to the risk. The persistent slowdown in IT industries in recent times has led to massive re-trenchment of computer engineers all over the world. Thus global-ization may have significant adverse impact on welfare by exposing citizens to greater economic risk. The possible gains from growth may be outweighed by the increased insecurity. This is particularly true of poor countries such as India, which do not have adequate social security arrangements.

It happens to be true that more than 95 per cent of the astronomical volume of daily foreign exchange transactions is for speculative pur-poses. This fantastic surge in speculation is a direct offshoot of the same IT revolution. Electronic technology can update information and transfer millions of dollars at nominal cost in a matter of seconds. Dismantling of capital controls in deference to globalization has left national governments nearly powerless to do anything about the capricious movement of short term capital or hot money. Uncontrol-lable speculation brought down the European Monetary System and caused meltdowns in Mexico, Russia, and countries of East Asia. These cases are discussed in detail in Chapter 5. The risk is particu-larly high if domestic financial institutions are not properly supervised.

Worsening of Distribution

The world suffers from appalling inequality in the distribution of income and wealth, both between and within countries. The World Development Report (1992) of the United Nation's Development Programme (UNDP) introduced the champagne glass as the graphic metaphor for the extreme inequality prevailing. The bowl of the glass represents the abundance enjoyed by the 20 per cent of the popula-tion living in the richest countries and enjoying 82 per cent of the world's income. At the bottom of the stem, where the sediment settles, survive the poorest 20 per cent on 1.4 per cent of total income. Combined income of the top 20 per cent is sixty times that of the bottom 20 per cent, a gap which has doubled since 1950.

Within the USA, the median family income was about the same in 1995 as it was in 1973. But over the same period the rich have become a great deal richer and the poor significantly poorer. The remunera-tion of the chief executives of large corporations has more than qua-drupled in real terms (Krugman 1998). The pattern is more or less similar for other countries too. Everywhere the skilled–unskilled wage gap has widened, reflecting the skill-biased, highly capital-intensive nature of technological change of the past decades. Distri-bution of wealth is even worse than that of income.

Although it will certainly be wrong to put the blame entirely on the forces of liberalization and globalization for the miserable state of affairs in distribution, it is undeniable that reduction of control over market forces and diminished power of governments to tax the rich will exacerbate the trend. For the sake of fiscal discipline, neoliberalism will not hesitate to do away with welfare programmes targeting the deprived and the underprivileged. Without question, such programmes have often failed to achieve their objectives, but that can be a valid argument for reform, not abolition.

Deregulation and decontrol within the economy have great potential to become a socially disruptive force by widening the gap between the fortunes of the rich and the underprivileged. Ensuring equity in distribution has never been a strong point of the market mechanism, as is admitted even by its most ardent advocates. In the words of Ralph Nader, 'Deregulation has been a licence to profiteer and steal from workers, pension holders, and shareholders'. Economic growth may be a powerful tool for increasing a nation's wealth, but it cannot guarantee an equitable sharing of the fruits of that wealth. Here a vital space for intervention is left for the state.

Adverse Impact on the Environment and Cultural Diversity

The wasteful lifestyle of western consumerism is steadily becoming the universal model for all societies. Use of automobiles and other energy intensive appliances are spreading rapidly in the wake of globalization. Over the next decade a huge leap is projected in fossil fuel consumption for production and transportation, stimulated by the dismantling of barriers to trade and investment. Consideration for exhaustible resources and the environment in general cannot realistically be expected from a system where private profit is the driving force. For instance, less than 50 per cent of the automobile companies have any environmental policy and out of those who have less than 50 per cent have addressed the environmental aspect of the product in the policy. National governments have the collective responsibility to look beyond their immediate interest of attaining international competitiveness and take a long term, global view of environmental issues.

Another highly undesirable effect of the spread of a universal model is the progressive disappearance of local values and cultures. The days seem to be approaching when every place will look and feel like every place else, with the same glass-and-steel towers, the same shopping malls offering the same products to the prototypical consumer and the same streets crowded with the same cars. ('The consumer is as much a mass produced commodity as cornflakes or Coca Cola.') Is this a better life? Business could not care less, and business, as even a child knows today, is the supreme authority who holds the answer to everything.

ROLE OF THE STATE

Contrary to the claims of the neoliberals, economic reform cannot be reduced to the simple formula of a minimalist state. Avoiding crude intervention like that of the past, the state must allow almost full freedom to private agents in the ordinary affairs of day-to-day business. Nevertheless, it must keep a close watch on such activities to prevent abuse of private monopoly power. The consequences will be disastrous if decontrol simply translates into a change from inefficient state management to unrestricted exploitation of economic power. This is the central theme that will be repeated all through this book.

The lacklustre performance of public sector enterprises the world over has demonstrated that absence of competition kills incentive for innovation and generates sloth and slack. It is thus detrimental to public interest. But in order to have positive welfare effects, competition must be effective. There must be a number of agents actively engaged in competition against each other. Also, the field must be open for potential entrants. Active rivalry among incumbents plus threat of entry by outsiders constitute effective competition. Some economists call it a contestable market. Effective competition or contestability is good for a society, because it promotes allocative efficiency by bringing prices in line with costs and removes internal inefficiency or slack by putting pressure on managers and workers to perform.

The market, left to itself, will seldom fulfill the conditions of effective competition. It is in the self interest of private agents to destroy contestability through collusive arrangements (explicit or implicit) and other anticompetitive practices of a myriad variety. The much vaunted market discipline is an empty concept without effective competition. The state's indispensable role is to maintain effective competition in the system through appropriate measures that do not kill off private initiative in the process. Liberalization and globalization can only be deemed a success from the social point of view if they improve effective competition in the system. Otherwise, they may fail to produce any long lasting gain. The massive British privatization programme, widely acclaimed as an economic and political success, has been seriously flawed on this count. Too often it stopped with a transfer of ownership without any backup action to introduce contestability. (Chapter 3 treats this issue in detail.)

When external effects are significantly present in production or consumption, the market mechanism fails to attain efficiency. In particular, free global competition cannot guarantee optimum use of air, water, forests, energy, and other environmental resources for development sustainable over a long horizon as there is no automatic mechanism for internalizing the social externality costs. Carefully designed policies are needed to prevent overexploitation and to preserve ecological balance. (The matter is treated in Chapters 2 and 3.)

Let us consider a small sample of some highly topical questions that any student of social science is likely to encounter repeatedly in this era. (Often friends and even strangers would turn to him for answers, suggestions, and guidance.)

1. Should giant multinationals be allowed unrestricted entry into our country? Is foreign capital an unmitigated evil?
2. Should government regulation of economic activity be totally done away with?
3. What really happened in East Asia in 1997–8 and why?
4. What is the case for privatization in a labour surplus country such as ours?
5. Will globalization necessarily ruin the environment? What can the government do to avert disaster?
6. What are sustainable development and green accounting? Trading in pollution permits?
7. How is industrial concentration measured and what is its link with efficiency?
8. What is the scope for introducing competition in public utilities and network industries? What should be the appropriate pricing rule?
9. What is 'new protectionism' in world trade?
10. Will the price of medicine soar out of reach of the common man under the new patent regime? What steps may the government take to check this?

The purpose of the present volume is to set out clearly the tangled issues surrounding questions such as these and sort them out systematically in the light of basic principles of economics.

OVERVIEW OF CHAPTERS

The second chapter explores the intimate link between economic activities and the environment. Major topics covered include green accounting, sustainable development, scope and limitations of government regulation in environmental protection, and the close link between the environment and expansion of global business.

The neoliberal ideology that swept the world after the collapse of communism has mounted a massive assault on the developmental state on all fronts. After a decade of retreat, however, there are unmistakable signs that the state is gradually coming back into the drama of development again. Chapter 3 tries to put the role of the state in an economic system in proper perspective. Theory and practice of regulation are subjected to close scrutiny with special emphasis on competition policies that attempt to promote social welfare by increasing the contestability of markets. Deregulation of network industries and the associated problems of optimal pricing are examined. Privatization as a policy option is scrutinized in detail.

Globalization is inextricably tied up with the expansion of global business conducted by MNCs. Eschewing passion, Chapter 4 makes an attempt to take a look at the complex role played by such corporations in today's world.

Macroeconomic policy coordination has always posed serious problems for an economy open to foreign trade and investment. The difficulty has increased manifold in a world where the trend is for the removal of restrictions on the movement of short term finance across national boundaries. Autonomy of national governments with respect to domestic policy is under serious threat. Chapter 5 summarizes an enormous literature to highlight the basic issues.

One paradoxical and disturbing feature of the international economy is that along with the move towards a multilateral, liberalized trading order, protectionism has also been steadily on the rise in the past quarter century. Both industrialized as well as developing countries are vigorous players in this game. The multifarious tools of protectionism and the formation of regional trading blocs in violation of multilateralism are the subject of Chapter 6.

Chapter 7 traces the long and rather uneven road the developing countries have traversed from the General Agreement on Tariffs and Trade (GATT 1947) to Doha. Issues of special relevance to their welfare—expansion of trade and the plight of unskilled labour, trade-related intellectual property (TRIPS), and the price of medicine, for example—are examined in detail.

Chapter 8 concludes the book with some general remarks on the pros and cons of the new world order.

This book is not an exhaustive treatment of liberalization and globalization. The focus is mainly on the non-financial sectors. Comprehensive discussion of financial reform is absent, but the need for adequate regulation in this vital area has been duly stressed in the proper contexts.

TWO

Economic Activity
and the Environment

After delineating the crucial role of environmental resources in the economic process this chapter moves on to the major theme of 'market failure' caused by external effects and the various solutions that have been proposed to deal with it. The device of tradable pollution permits and the property rights solution associated with Ronald Coase get detailed attention. The close links between the forces of globalization and the environment are explored in depth. The valuation issue of environmental resources, the Kuznets Curve, and the idea of sustainable development are briefly discussed.

ENVIRONMENT AND THE ECONOMY

The familiar circular flow diagram, which invariably appears in the first chapter of every introductory economics text, shows the interaction between two broadly defined sectors of the economy, firms (producers) and households (consumers). The firm sells goods and services to the households and purchases inputs or factor services from them. The system is in equilibrium when demands and supplies match in the markets for all goods and services and factor inputs. There are no factors that are not owned by the households. The environment simply acts as a passive backdrop, playing no essential role in the process of production, exchange, or distribution.

In recent years, however, a concern has been growing rapidly about the impact of economic activities on the environment. This has led to the incorporation of a third sector, the environment, in the

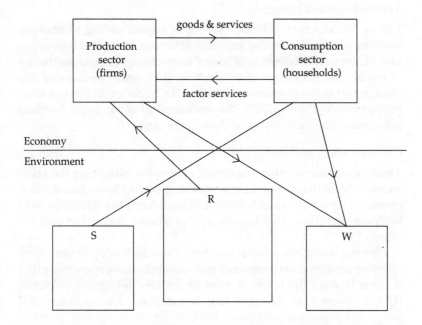

Figure 2.1: Economy–Environment Interaction

traditional circular flow diagram. The expanded system is shown in Figure 2.1.

The three boxes in the lower half, designated S, R, and W, indicate the three major economic functions of the environment. S stands for the direct services supplied in the form of living and recreational space and natural beauty; R for the mineral, forest, and water resources used in the production process and W symbolizes the role of the environment as the sink for all the waste products generated in the acts of production, distribution, and consumption.

PROTECTIVE MEASURES

The traditional preoccupation with growth has not paid any attention to the adverse impact of economic activities on the environment. Services of most natural resources were treated as practically limitless in supply and, hence, costless. But with the growth of concern about the environment, measures have been taken to mitigate the harmful impact. They are broadly of two types:

Technological Change

Just as introduction of labour saving or capital saving technology leads to a reduction in the amounts of labour or capital inputs per unit of output, the adoption of 'clean' technologies can reduce the use of environmental factors in production. It is mostly because of this change that in the developed countries (DCs) pollution has not risen proportionately with GNP. The emissions of some major harmful substances have actually gone down over time.

Conservation and Recycling

These constitute another important means for protecting the environment from the onslaught of economic growth. Once again the rich countries have put in much effort to design items in such a way as to facilitate recycling. This has already produced noticeable positive effects.

Unfortunately, the adoption of both clean technologies and more effective conservation methods involves substantial expenditure that is often beyond the reach of most of the less developed countries (LDCs). There is at the same time less demand for environmental protection in such economies as the taste for environmental services is positively associated with the level of affluence of a community. Income elasticity of the environment is fairly high.

The Environmental Kuznets Curve encapsulates a direct connection between the environment and the income of an economy. It is an inverted U-shaped relation between pollution and income. (A similar relation between income and inequality was previously studied by Simon Kuznets, hence the name.) At low levels of development pollution tends to rise more than proportionately with growth, above a certain level this is reversed. In the early stages of growth there is heavy investment in industries and within the industrial sector itself the bias is toward heavy and chemical industries. Anti-pollution measures are either non-existent or very weak. Therefore, the rate of growth of pollution often exceeds the rate of growth of GNP. In advanced stages of development pollution control measures are much more effective and at the same time the shift of economic activities from industry to services leads to a sharp reduction in the energy intensity of production. Unfortunately, the Kuznets Curve is not quite comforting enough to rest on. Even if the pollution intensity of a country falls, its total level of pollution may continue to rise. For example, although emission of carbon dioxide per US$ 100 of national income has declined in the USA, total emission of carbon dioxide has gone on rising over time. Danger to the atmosphere is not diminished if the total cannot be brought down.

Interestingly, there is evidence that at least for some pollutants such as carbon dioxide the turning point of the curve is occurring at lower incomes. This lowering of the peak shows that several factors are working in favour of more rapid change to a cleaner environment in LDCs. These factors include quicker diffusion of cleaner production processes and abatement technologies, and a greater awareness of the costs of environmental damage.

GREEN ACCOUNTING

Concern for the environment has induced rethinking on many concepts and techniques used by applied economists including national income accounting. Conventional GNP is not an adequate measure of sustainable economic welfare by which we mean the flow of goods and services that can be currently produced without reducing future productive capacity, that is, without compromising the well-being of future generations. The value of timber cut down or minerals extracted is included in GNP but the resulting deforestation or loss of scarce natural resources and destruction of natural beauty are not given any consideration. This depreciation of environmental capital deserves to be treated at par with depreciation of physical capital. Among the classical economists Alfred Marshall emphasized the importance of natural capital and its proper use. Also, some expenditures are incurred purely to mitigate environmental damage (for example, those undertaken by households situated near highways or airports to reduce the level of noise pollution, or to counter the effect of smoke belched by a nearby factory). These protective expenditures add to current GNP but should be excluded from any measure of sustainable welfare because they do not reflect any increase in economic welfare. Taking all these factors, plus the volume of pollution not corrected by preventive measures (residual pollution), into account we arrive at the Index of Sustainable Economic Welfare (ISEW).

ISEW = GNP – (depreciation of physical capital + protective expenditure + depreciation of environmental capital + value of residual pollution)

The effect of this type of adjustment can be quite dramatic. One study for the UK showed that 2.1 per cent average annual growth in real GNP per capita over the period 1950–90 collapsed to a mere 0.1 per cent average annual growth in terms of ISEW.

REGULATORY MEASURES FOR NEGATIVE EXTERNALITY

Pollution is a harmful or negative externality. An externality is said to be present when the action of one agent directly affects the utility or the opportunity set of another. Such effects are typically unpriced and as a result markets often fail to achieve social efficiency in their presence. Profit maximizing firms attach weight only to private benefits or costs, but externalities create divergence between private and social magnitudes. Therefore, there is need for intervention in the market economy to bring the activities of self-seeking agents in line with the social optimum. In other words, externalities justify state regulation by causing 'market failure'. Such regulation, however, requires much information that is not easily available, consumes resources and, worse, the regulators may lack the motivation to

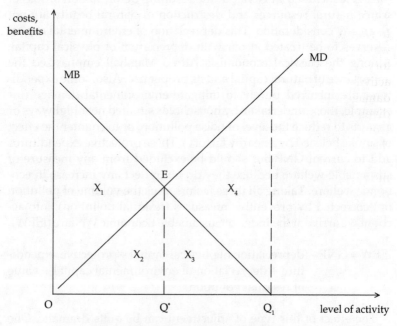

Figure 2.2: Optimum Level of Pollution

promote public interest. Chapter 3 deals with these problems in more detail. We abstract from them here.

A simple figure can be used to illustrate market failure and the need for government action. In Figure 2.2 marginal damage through pollution caused by some particular activity is shown as the upward rising MD curve. The marginal net (private) benefit to the polluter is the other curve MB. The benefit is revenue less private costs. The socially optimum level of activity is Q^*, where the difference between benefit and social cost (private cost of polluter plus damage cost of the victim) is maximum. The associated optimal pollution level is Q^*E (note that it is not zero). The free market solution is Q_1 where MB is zero (revenue minus private cost is maximum). The activity level is beyond the social optimum.

Now let us take up the various direct and indirect (market-based) regulatory measures that are usually adopted.

Direct regulation involves setting of minimum acceptable standards for emissions. The polluter is simply forbidden to carry on his activity beyond Q^*.

Market based solutions take the following forms.

Merger (Internalization of Externality)

In some cases of producer–producer externality, merger is a viable way of overcoming the problem. Suppose that the polluter is a factory and the victim is a laundry. If the two units merge, the optimum activity level will be cut back to Q^*, because now the pollution damage is included in the firm's own cost. The source of inefficiency, divergence between private and social costs, has been eliminated. Unfortunately, the merger solution does not work in many cases. In the situation involving a noisy highway and neighbouring residents, for example. There is also the danger that merger may increase monopoly power in the market place. The welfare loss on this count may offset the gain resulting from the internalization of the externality.

Taxation

If an appropriate tax is imposed on the polluter then his private cost will be brought in line with social cost and it will give him incentive to contract production toward the optimum. In the figure, a tax (per unit) of amount Q^*E will shift MB down and make it pass through Q^*.

The problem with this approach (now associated with the name of the classical economist, Arthur Pigou) is that the government should have adequate information about the benefits and costs of pollution so that the tax amount can be precisely calculated. This is very unlikely to be true in all but the simplest of cases. Actually, placing a monetary value on social benefits and costs of any activity can be extremely problematic. It is the unavailability or inadequacy of information that forces regulatory agencies to go for quantitative restrictions or standards setting.

Tradable Permits

This is a combination of market and non-market measures that is more efficient than simple setting of standards. Each polluter is assigned a permit to emit effluent up to a limit (say 100 tonnes). But the individual permits can be traded within the overall limit set. The firms which are able to meet the standard at lower cost will benefit by selling part of their permits to firms which find it too expensive to meet those standards. Efficiency improves in the sense that cost of production is lower compared to what it would otherwise be consistent with the overall environmental constraints.

Suppose there are only two firms, A and B, each with a permit of 100 tonnes. The overall standard is 200 tonnes. (We assume that the informational problems have somehow been solved to arrive at this value of the desired volume of pollution.) Firm A with cleaner technology can produce its optimum output emitting only 80 tonnes; whereas B's chosen output will create effluents of 120 tonnes. If permits were not tradable B would either have to curtail production or incur extra abatement costs to keep within 100 tonnes. Suppose this abatement cost is Rs 500. Then if A sells its 20 unused units to B for (say) Rs 400 both parties will be better off and the total social cost of meeting the target of 200 tonnes will be lower. Unlike regulations which give producers no incentive to do better than the required minimum, now the 'cleaner' firms have incentive to more than meet the target and exchange the 'surplus' for cash. Here the distribution of pollution is market determined although the overall total is regulated.

Permit trading is practised in many countries. The Tennessee Valley Authority in the USA has agreed to buy allowances to emit 10,000 tonnes of sulphur dioxide, an agent of acid rain, from private companies. It is less expensive than installing 'scrubbers' to meet sulphur emission standards or to change capital equipment to switch to harder, lower sulphur coal and other compatible inputs.

The Bargaining or Property Rights Solution

The basic idea, associated with the name of Ronald Coase, is that if property rights are clearly assigned then, under certain conditions, private negotiation may lead to the socially efficient solution.

An asset is deemed to be private property if three kinds of rights are associated with its ownership: the right of use including the right to exclude others from its use, the right to any income generated, and the right to transfer ownership. Some rights, such as citizenship, do not have the last feature. They are inalienable.

Let us look at Figure 2.2 again. Coase's argument is that at Q_1 there is a big incentive for the victim to make a deal with the polluter. If production is cut back from Q_1 to Q^* the gain to the victim (reduction in damage) is given by the sum of the areas X_3 and X_4. This is the area under the MD curve between the two activity levels. But the loss to the polluter for the same move is the area under MB, which is X_3. Since his gain exceeds this loss, it will pay the victim to offer a payment to the polluter to restrict output to Q^*, the social optimum. This is the situation when the polluter has the right to pollute, but chooses not to exercise it to the full extent (up to Q_1) as he gets compensated for choosing Q^* instead. Now consider the other case where the victim has the right to clean air. His most preferred position is at the origin, with zero pollution. This again is socially sub-optimal. But this time the producer can offer him a payment to be willing to accept Q^*. His loss from the proposed move is X_2, which is smaller than the polluter's gain, $X_1 + X_2$. So the mutually beneficial move is feasible, with the burden of compensation falling on the polluter.

Although our notion of justice demands that it is the polluter who should pay compensation, the reverse case may cease to seem outrageous once it is noted that the victim may be the wealthier party. Actually the principle of 'victim pays' is already in operation. Sweden pays (and assists in other ways) Poland to reduce acid rain. The Montreal Protocol contains provisions under which India, China, and other developing nations are to be compensated by richer countries for restricting their use of chlorofluorocarbons (CFCs) that damage the ozone layer. Some developed countries have agreed to pay Brazil for desisting from overexploiting its tropical rainforests. In the 1992 UN Conference on Environment and Development (the Earth Summit) held in Rio de Janeiro the DCs wanted uniform global standards for environmental regulation. This was very strongly opposed by the developing countries who blamed the past actions of the DCs for the present state of environmental degradation and demanded heavy compensation for compliance with regulations that are too severe from their point of view.

The Coase Theorem: Resource allocation is socially efficient so long as there is a clear assignment of property rights and cost of negotiating and enforcing transactions is zero.

Striking as the result is, it is critically dependent upon its assumptions. Even when property rights are well specified the theorem fails whenever transaction costs (associated with getting all the parties together, finding the optimal solution, and conducting negotiations) are substantial. This is likely to be the case when a large number of persons is involved. (Can you imagine the Coase solution for the problem of vehicular pollution in Kolkata or Mumbai?) Even if the number of parties is small, bargaining can fail under partial or imperfect information. Overestimating the opponent's gain, one may press too hard.

Transactions costs can be broadly classified as:

1. Search and information acquisition costs are incurred for ascertaining the extent and nature of the damage for the victims and also fixing the perpetrator's responsibility as accurately as possible.

2. Bargaining costs are those involving money, time, and effort needed to get the parties together and to arrive at an agreement.

3. Contracting costs are those associated with drawing up legal documents in support of the agreement.

4. Enforcement costs are for monitoring that the polluter is indeed honouring the contract. Non-compliance calls for punishment or further negotiation. This entails substantial cost.

Coase's result requires all these costs to be negligible. In reality that is not even approximately the case.

Besides, the burden of negative externalities today often extends to unborn generations. It is not clear who will represent them in a Coasian bargain.

THE VALUATION PROBLEM

Let us turn to the very important issue of valuation. To devise effective methods for controlling the problem of negative externalities some way must be found of placing monetary value on social costs and benefits of an activity or an amenity. Economists have come up with three broad methods. The 'stated preference method' uses answers to questionnaires used in surveys designed to elicit peoples' willingness to pay (WTP) for the maintenance of some environmental good. The 'revealed preference method' is based on the idea that even though some amenity is not priced directly in the market, consumption of its service may need complementary input of some other priced private goods. For example, access to a natural park may be free but individuals will have to incur travel costs in money and time to get there. Expenditure on the marketed good (travel) will be a good proxy for WTP for the services of the park. The third method, 'hedonic pricing', observes the variations caused in market prices by variations in the supply of environmental goods and estimates the value of benefits therefrom. For example, WTP for reduction in noise pollution may be inferred from the price premium commanded by houses located at greater distance from airports.

A survey carried out in 1995 by a team from the Indira Gandhi Institute of Development Research (IGIDR), Mumbai, interviewed more than five hundred residents of Mumbai to find out the willingness of the community to contribute for an autonomous organization that would be responsible for the maintenance of the Borivli National Park, a wilderness area of 110 sq km that is home to several hundred species of flora and fauna. Mean WTP was calculated to be Rs 7.50 per family per month. The net present value (at an appropriate rate of discount) of the contribution toward preservation of the park came to Rs 1030 million. The study revealed that poorer sections of the people, who could not afford to make monetary contributions, were willing to contribute labour time for work on maintenance. A similar project by the Flood Hazard Research Centre in the UK had estimated earlier that in 1987–8 people were willing to pay £ 14–18 per household per annum in taxes to protect recreational beaches from erosion.

Willingness to contribute for preservation of some environmental amenity is not confined to its actual users alone. Even non-users express such willingness. This is a measure of the existence value of the amenity. When Prince William Sound, Alaska, was devastated by the Exxon Valdez oil spill in 1989, the WTP of non-users to avoid such damage in future worked out to no less than US$ 31 per US household. Another notion, the option value of a resource, is the estimated value as a source of new, as yet unknown, uses in future. The three values, current use, future use, and existence, define the total economic value of a resource:

Total Economic Value = use value + option value + existence value.

GLOBALIZATION AND THE ENVIRONMENT

Greater integration of the world economy through heightened trade and investment flows and greater mobility of factors will impact on the environment in three major ways:

Scale Effect

Since the scale of activities is transformed from the small and local to large and global, particularly in the export sectors, this may add seriously to environmental degradation in countries specializing in environment-intensive activities like mining, forestry, fishing, wood products, and industrial chemicals. Moreover, environmental sustainability is impossible without accountability, which is best ensured at a local level. In a global system where close contact between the investors and the local community is lost it may be difficult to keep environmental damage in check. Higher economic growth, on the other hand, should enable governments to raise resources through taxation and other means for the abatement of pollution. This, however, will take time and governments in LDCs may have other more pressing priorities for the use of tax revenues.

By reducing barriers to foreign investment, globalization has enabled MNCs such as Exxon and Shell (oil), Rio Tinto Zinc and BHP (mining), Pescanova and Arctic–Tyson Foods (fishing), Boise Cascade and Mitsubishi (logging), Cargill and Monsanto (food), to name just a few at random, to expand their operations around the world. Since the primary objectives are profits and growth, adverse environmental side effects of activities are often not given due consideration.

Technique Effect

If greater integration provides access to cleaner techniques and if such techniques are widely adopted then noticeable improvement on the environment front may be expected.

Composition Effect

If it succeeds in raising a country's income, global integration may shift consumer demand toward relatively cleaner goods and services and greater international exposure is likely to enhance the value placed on environmental protection. The rate of growth needs to attain a critical level, however, before this effect can really make itself felt. Meanwhile, the logic of specialization according to comparative advantage may dictate a switch in many parts of the developing world towards less environment-friendly activities.

Empirical evidence on this question is mixed. Some studies have shown that energy use per unit of GNP in the former centrally planned economies declined sharply after market reform. Energy intensity in China reportedly fell by 30 per cent between 1985 and 1997. Several countries such as Indonesia, Turkey, and Costa Rica, on the other hand, showed increased pollution following trade liberalization mostly due to the expansion of some polluting activities.

One phenomenon that is causing some concern is that in the regime of heightened global competition nations are now tempted to lower environmental (and labour) standards as part of strategy for attracting new investment or for preventing footloose capital from moving elsewhere. A race to the bottom is thus set up. Countries with stiffer environmental regulation feel threatened and their protectionist lobbies acquire more clout. There is, however, not much evidence that location of production units by MNCs has been significantly influenced by the existence of such pollution havens. It remains true nonetheless that lower labour and environmental standards do form a prominent part of the concessional package held out by LDCs to foreign investors, particularly in their special export processing zones (EPZ) or free trade zones (FTZ). A controversial FTZ containing more than 3000 factories known as *maquiladoras* is located in Mexico on the border with the USA. In China, too, numerous FTZs are in operation in the provinces of Guandong and Fujian, where wages are low and environmental standards rather lax.

The palm oil industry of Malaysia provides an interesting example of adapting successfully to both outward orientation and environmental protection. Compliance is high yet price in the competitive export market could be kept stable because development of commercial by-products through state-funded research helped generate additional revenues on a substantial scale. Examples such as this, unfortunately, are not very common, particularly in the poorer countries of the world.

The heightened forces of market competition tend to undermine ecological best practice in developing nations in another way. IMF–World Bank structural adjustment assistance is strictly conditional on reduced government spending. Many such countries have chosen to slash expenditure on environmental protection. For example, between 1986 and 1989 budget for the Mexican environmental protection agency was cut by 60 per cent in real terms and in Brazil, in 1998,

BOX 2.1: Mexico's maquiladoras

Among the world's best documented FTZs, Mexico's maquiladoras consist mainly of US-owned factories that import materials from the USA for assembly and re-export. They are the country's second largest foreign exchange earner, after oil. In 1989 total export earnings were no less than US$ 3 billion. Even before the formation of the North American Free Trade Agreement (NAFTA—a trading bloc consisting of the USA, Canada, and Mexico) no Mexican duties were charged on imports and the USA taxed only the value added.

The maquiladoras provide poor working and living conditions and labour organizations are prohibited. Little attention is paid to health and safety regulations. An examination of a randomly selected sample of 12 US-owned firms in 1993 revealed that not a single one was obeying Mexican environmental law. The average productive working life is ten years and employee turnover is fairly high. There is evidence to believe that there may be collusion between the Mexican government and the official Mexican trade union movement to keep workers unorganized in the maquiladoras.

The factories are supposed to return waste material to the USA, from where most raw materials are imported. But in reality a very small percentage is actually returned. According to one report the units are unable to account for 95 per cent of the waste they generated between 1969 and 1989. While more than a thousand generated hazardous waste, only 307 had official licence.

In the mid-1990s, high levels of pollutants were detected outside the plants including drainage water containing xylene, an industrial solvent, at concentrations 6000 times the US standard. Pollution related diseases were steadily on the rise in the region, on both sides of the border. In March 1993 twenty-seven families of Brownsville, Texas, filed lawsuits against eighty-eight maquillas in Matamoros. Among the accused were companies associated with familiar multinationals such as General Motors, Union Carbide, Fisher Price, and Zenith Electronics.

Source: Goldsmith and Mander (2001).

funds dedicated to protecting the Amazonian rain forests were reduced from US$ 61.1 million to US$ 6.4 million as part of a general policy of expenditure reduction. An advertisement placed in *Fortune* magazine by the Philippine government said, 'To attract companies like yours ... we have felled mountains, razed jungles, filled swamps, moved rivers, relocated towns ... all to make it easier for you and your business to do business here'.

The appalling gas tragedy of Bhopal, in which 6000 lives were lost and another 200,000 suffered crippling disabilities, also points clearly to what can happen when a giant MNC adopts industrial safety standards far below the level acceptable in the advanced countries.

The industrialized countries themselves are beginning to feel the bite of intensified competition. In 1995 the MNC, Boise Cascade, threatened to relocate some of its operations to Mexico in protest against stiff US environmental protection standards. Actually, earlier that year it had closed mills in Oregon and Idaho and set up production in Guerrero, Mexico, to take advantage of new investment opportunities. 'How many more mills will be closed', a company spokesman said, 'will depend on what the Congress does'. That same year action was taken to make US timber producers more competitive by opening up national forests to deregulated logging at subsidized rates.

In 1996 the Canadian government introduced legislation banning the import of MMT—a neurotoxin used as a fuel additive that seriously damages pollution control systems of vehicles. Immediately the sole North American producer of MMT, Ethyl Corporation of the USA, sued the Canadian government US$ 350 million in damages, claiming among other things that merely by introducing and debating the bill the Canadian authorities had done irreparable damage to its international reputation. The government's action was held to be tantamount to an 'expropriation of future profits'. Eventually the ban was lifted and a hefty compensation plus an apology were given.

Protectionist groups in the developed countries keep on demanding strong trade sanctions against countries, mostly in Asia and Africa, that have lax standards of environmental protection, claiming that it is making the playing field slanted against them. This view is flawed because it ignores some basic differences among the nations of the world. Countries may have widely divergent attitudes towards environmental protection (or labour standards for that matter) depending on differences in income levels, the absorption capacity of their ecosystems, and in cultural values. The GATT recognizes this and does not allow unilateral imposition of domestic standards on trading partners. The USA at one time banned tuna imports from Mexico on the ground that Mexican fishermen did not use the dolphin-friendly nets required by US regulation. A GATT panel ruled against the USA on this issue. This underscores the point that trade policy (tariff, quota, or outright ban) is almost never the appropriate policy to deal with environment related issues. Only when the distortion originates in foreign trade that trade policy measures can serve as

---

BOX 2.2: ISO 14001 Standards for Environmental Management

The International Organization for Standards based in Geneva publishes voluntary standards for technology and business activity. It has developed ISO 14001 as a tool for efficient environmental management. The worldwide growth in environmental awareness has caused certification to jump twenty-fold between 1995 and 1997. Firms seeking certification are required to take the following steps:

1. an initial review by management to identify issues of concern;
2. determination of priorities for action, taking local environmental regulation into account;
3. preparation of an environmental policy statement and development of performance targets based on that statement (for example, reduction of emissions by a specified amount over a specified period);
4. implementation of the environmental management system with defined procedures and responsibilities;
5. implementation review, performance measurement, and management audits.

Not surprisingly, firms in the DCs have taken out the bulk of the certificates issued so far. This is a reflection of the high demand for environmentally responsible management in these countries. But more and more developing countries are coming forward to obtain a greater share of the certificates. In 1997 the ten nations topping the list for the industrialized world were: Japan (713), Germany (352), Denmark (347), Netherlands (263), Austria (198), Sweden (194), Switzerland (170), Finland (151), Australia (137), Belgium (137), and Italy (103). For Asia the toppers were: South Korea (463), Taiwan (183), Singapore (65), Thailand (61), Hong Kong, China (46), Indonesia (45), Turkey (44), Malaysia (36), India (28), and China (22). For Latin America the top three were: Brazil (63), Argentina (28), and Mexico (11).

In 1997 a total of 5017 certificates were given to fifty-three countries. The corresponding figures for 1995 were 257 for eighteen countries.

Source: UNCTAD Reports.

---

effective, first best instruments. Environment related externalities do not fall in this category. This argument, however, valid as it is in its own context, does not destroy the strategic utility of trade policy to environmentalists, because such policy can be used to force reluctant governments to adopt measures that tackle environmental problems at their source.

Trade policy can affect the environment by changing the composition of exports and imports. When the USA imposed restrictions on the number of cars that could be imported from Japan in the 1980s, the Japanese exporters shifted from small to more expensive larger cars to maximize the value per car. Since these cars had lower fuel-efficiency the average volume of pollution by imported cars went up.

Export controls can be an effective tool for protecting scarce resources, but they often run foul of trade rules of the new international economic order. When the Canadian Fisheries Act prohibited export of unprocessed salmon and herring it was challenged by the USA and the Act was struck down by an international panel. Restrictions on raw log exports also have very slim chance of survival.

Over the past couple of decades several multilateral environment agreements (MEA) have been signed. The prominent ones are the Basle Convention (control of transboundary movement of hazardous wastes), the Montreal Protocol (regulation of trade in products harmful to the ozone layer), the Kyoto Protocol (regulation of greenhouse gas emissions by DCs), Convention on Biological Diversity (CBD), the Framework Convention on Climate Change (FCCC), and the North American Agreement on Environmental Cooperation (NAAEC). There are proposals for the creation of a World Environmental Organization (WEO) to act as a forum for bargaining and negotiations, which will not be confined to national governments only. It would also mobilize international support for domestic groups working to improve compliance with environment policy.

To get an idea of the formidable problems that an agency like the WEO will face, we note that the US Congress prevented ratification of the Kyoto Protocol that mandates the country to reduce its greenhouse gas emissions drastically by 2012. The argument is that such a move would damage the US economy, causing exodus of capital to the developing countries who are exempted from the mandate. In 1992 the European Union (EU) had refused to introduce a carbon tax on the ground that the competitiveness of domestic business would be undermined.

THE INDIAN SCENARIO AT A GLANCE

Environmental degradation in our country, particularly in the sprawling conurbations, has reached alarming proportions. The annual average levels of suspended particulate matters (SPM) is at least three times higher than WHO standards, with Delhi, Kolkata, and Kanpur recording levels over five times the standard. Unregulated growth of vehicular population has been a major contributory factor. The number jumped from 2.1 million registered vehicles in 1973 to 25.2 million in 1993. Among industries the major culprits are rubber, leather, and metal products, and industrial chemicals. The quality of our water resources has been severely degraded through discharge of domestic and industrial effluents.

The cost to the society in terms of mortality and disease has been incalculable. A World Bank study of thirty-six major cities and towns in 1995 estimated that air pollution alone accounts for 40,350 premature deaths, 19,805,000 hospital admissions, and 1200 million incidences of minor sickness annually.

The government of India's initiatives for pollution management are outlined in the National Water Policy (1987), the National Conservation Strategy and the Policy Statement on Environment and Development (1992), and the Policy Statement for Abatement of Pollution (1992). There are central as well as state Pollution Control Boards (PCBs) entrusted with the task of monitoring pollution and implementing remedial measures. But enforcement is often lax due to lack of resources and trained personnel and, more importantly, inability to withstand pressure from producers' groups opposed to the introduction of environment-friendly methods as it cuts into their profits. It is a typical case of capture of regulatory agencies by vested interests (see Chapter 3 for more on regulatory capture). Fortunately, owing to closer supervision by international agencies and greater awareness among the populace, implementation of environmental policies has taken a turn for the better in recent years.

THREE

Role of the State in the Economy

The aim of this chapter is to set a proper perspective on the function of the state in an era whose driving force is neoliberalism. Although neoliberalism in its extreme form is hardly worthy of attention, the traditional idea of a monolithic developmental state is also no longer relevant or tenable. The logic of intervention is set out in terms of the three basic causes of market failure—externalities, public goods (including common property resources), and monopoly power. In delineating the nature of public policy in imperfectly competitive markets the damaging possibility of 'government failure' caused by the agency problem of moral hazard is given due emphasis. A brief discussion of natural monopoly is followed by a treatment of the problem of regulation. The various dilemmas facing the regulator are spelt out to give an idea of the complexity of the task.

Liberalization without effective government action to promote contestability may be socially harmful. Appropriate competition policy to combat such anticompetitive practices as collusion and predatory pricing are outlined. Privatization as a tool of promoting efficiency is given detailed treatment. The chapter ends with a discussion of public sector reform and a case study of telecom decontrol in India.

Let us take a quick glance at the evolving role of the state over the last half century. The decades following World War II witnessed a great surge in state involvement the world over in the provision of goods and services. This was particularly prominent in the LDCs that had recently won independence from foreign rule and were bent on achieving rapid growth through a process of careful economic planning modelled on that of the Soviet Union. This was considered the only viable option, given the enormous scope for market failure in these backward economies. It was believed that direct control of important sectors would facilitate macromanagement. State intervention was also deemed necessary to bring about an equitable distribution of income and wealth. With the help of experts from the advanced countries, detailed sectoral as well as economy-wide plan models were formulated and in the process of implementation hardly any sphere of economic activity remained directly or indirectly untouched by the 'visible hand' of the state.

This trend has undergone a dramatic reversal since the 1980s. Moves to reduce the state's involvement in regulation and ownership have been proceeding apace in almost all countries irrespective of their stage of development. According to one World Bank report, between 1980 and 1995 some 18,000 state-owned enterprises were transferred to the private sector including 14,500 in the former communist countries and two thousand in LDCs. There was massive privatization in the UK under Margaret Thatcher, followed by France, Italy, New Zealand, Greece, and numerous other countries on a smaller scale.

Traditional economic theory used market-failure arguments to support the case of state intervention. Market failure implies the inability of self-interest driven market forces to achieve the social optimum. We have already encountered it in dealing with the problem of pollution. But the global record of poor performance in sectors under government control has led to a vigorous discussion of issues pertaining to what has come to be known as 'government failure'. Recent developments in economic theory explain this regulatory failure in terms of information and agency costs. Let us take up market failure first.

MARKET FAILURE

The major causes of market failure are:

Externalities

External effects (good or bad) create a divergence between private and social dimensions of the costs and benefits of economic activities. The free market works only with private values and, therefore, produces sub-optional results (overproduction for negative external effects, underprovision for positive ones). In Chapter 2 several ways were discussed of tackling a harmful externality, of which government intervention in the form of taxation is one. (A subsidy is required for a positive externality.) But as we noted, calculating the optimum tax requires a lot of information which the state is unlikely to possess. Also, tax administration is far from costless. It may cost an economy more than Re 1 to raise Re 1 of tax revenue. This is because in addition to the costs of collection there are further distortions in resource allocation caused by extra taxation. Poor information and/ or very costly administration will cause government failure to outweigh the market failure that was to be cured through taxation.

Public Goods

Public goods are characterized by one or both of the following features:

Non-rivalry in consumption

For a private good consumption by one individual precludes consumption (of the same unit) by another (for example, cake). A pure public good is one which can be simultaneously consumed by many in equal amounts (for example, street lighting, uncongested road, national defence)

Non-excludability/non-rejectability

Once the good is supplied to somebody it is impossible or very expensive to prevent others from consuming it (national defence, TV broadcasting to a great extent). This is non-excludability, whereas non-rejectability occurs when, once provided, a good has to be consumed by everybody, (noise, smog, acid rain are examples of such public bads)

A good may feature non-rivalry in consumption but still may be excludable. A film show or a cricket match are examples. Market provision of such goods is possible. It is the combination of non-rivalry plus non-excludability that frustrates the market by creating the 'free rider' problem. No consumer will be willing to pay for such a public good because once it is provided he cannot be prevented from enjoying its benefit. It is easy to see why no private party will be forthcoming to supply such a good. Similarly individual victims of pollution have incentive to understate their willingness to pay if asked to contribute to a common fund that will be used to compensate the polluter for curtailing his emissions. Therefore, unless the state steps in public goods will be underprovided or not provided at all and public bads that are often the by-product of market activities will tend to proliferate.

But note that the government also will have to face the free rider problem. To determine the socially optimum level of provision the consumers' true valuation of the goods need to be known but, as previously noted, individuals will understate their willingness to pay if they know they are going to be taxed in proportion to what they reveal. Equally, they will tend to overstate if their payment is not directly related to the amount provided.

Natural resources that are characterized by non-excludability but do not have the attribute of non-rivalry are called common property resources (CPR). An example is the stock of fish in a lake where the fish population has reached such a level that one fisherman's catch reduces that of others. Similarly, a forest becomes a CPR when one person's tree felling reduces the opportunity for others. Thus private activity has a social cost. Since the typical agent does not have to pay for this, he will push his activity (fishing or tree felling) to the point of zero marginal private benefit. Since everybody does the same, the CPR will get exhausted at a rate which exceeds the social optimum. This is known as the 'tragedy of the commons'. Allocation and enforcement of property rights will theoretically solve the problem, but fixing property rights on forests, lakes, rivers, or air may be very difficult, if not impossible. Hence the need for state regulation. Traditionally, it has been the local communities that have done the regulation with a high degree of efficiency. Their task was easier because the number of agents was smaller and each agent acted on a limited scale. Now population pressure is more intense and local agents have been joined by commercially motivated outsiders utilizing mechanical means of exploitation that are highly efficient for their private interests.

International commons of current interest include the high seas, Antarctica, deep seabed minerals, the electromagnetic spectrum, the stratospheric ozone layer, the global climatic system, outer space, and the endangered species on earth. Owing chiefly to the tireless campaigning by environmentalists all over the world, considerable effort is now being devoted to the design and implementation of mechanisms to constrain and coordinate the exploitation of these resources by individual countries.

Monopoly Power

A competitive industry produces the socially optimal output (in the absence of external effects) because in competitive equilibrium price (P) equals marginal cost (MC). This is optimal because P represents the consumers' WTP for an extra unit. When P > MC, output should be expanded because marginal benefit to consumers exceeds marginal cost and it should be reduced when P < MC. The optimum is reached when the two are equal. When the industry is under the control of a single seller, output is lower and price higher compared to the competitive benchmark. This is so because profit maximization calls for marginal revenue (MR) = MC and P > MR for imperfect competition. The competitive price–quantity combination is shown as (P_c, Q_c) and that under monopoly as (P_m, Q_m) in Figure 3.1. For simplicity MC is assumed to be constant. This will also equal average cost (AC) if fixed cost is zero. If fixed cost is positive, AC will exceed the constant MC. (Use the function C = F + cq to verify.)

For the competitive market structure producer's surplus (PS), defined as the excess of revenue over variable cost, is zero and consumers' surplus (CS) equals the area (A + B + C). Under monopoly CS is A and PS is B. B is a transfer from consumers to producers. The sum (CS + PS) is usually taken to be the measure of social welfare created by a particular industry. (Sometimes the social welfare is written as W = αCS + PS, $\alpha > 1$, giving more weight to the consumers' welfare. We shall use the more common form that gives equal weights.) By this

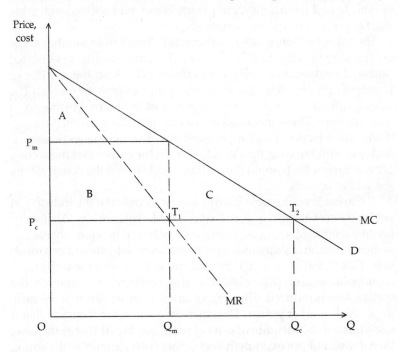

Figure 3.1: Monopoly Welfare Loss

criterion the welfare loss (WL) from monopoly is represented by area C. With linear demand and constant MC, C= B/2. Since B is profit (π_m) of the monopolist we have the result WL = π_m/2. With more general demand and cost functions the relationship between supernormal profit and monopoly welfare loss will not be so simple.

Any market structure in which P exceeds MC will produce a suboptimal level of output. This is true also in oligopolistic markets with a few large sellers because in equilibrium a gap persists between P and MC, although it is smaller than in monopoly. As the number of sellers increases oligopoly approaches perfect competition. This result plus a welfare ranking of market structures are contained in the Appendix. Another problem engendered by lack of competitive pressure is that the monopolist may lose the urge to minimize costs. 'The best of monopoly profits is a quiet life'. This is known as internal inefficiency or cost inefficiency or X-inefficiency. Under this type of inefficiency the cost curve in Figure 3.1 will not reflect the true cost to society of the resources used in the monopoly and hence P = MC will not give the social optimum. State monopolies are particularly vulnerable to cost inefficiency, but private companies with considerable market power are also not immune.

The theory of contestable markets casts doubt from another angle on the simple story told by Figure 3.1. Contestability asserts that potential competition may put an effective check on the exercise of monopoly power even if there is actually one seller in the market. The role of sunk cost is crucial. Certain costs must be incurred before entry into a market. These include the cost of establishing production and distribution facilities and advertising and promotional expenses associated with building up a reputation. To the extent that these costs are unrecoverable (should the entrant decide to exit the activity) they are said to be sunk.

A market is contestable if firms can enter or leave the industry at negligible cost at short notice. That is if sunk costs are low. Airlines or oceanic shipment are good examples, because it is relatively easy to switch routes, and ships and aeroplanes can be sold off without much loss. This threat of potential hit and run entry forces the incumbent monopolist to keep price close to average cost and consequently the welfare loss is reduced. Thus high market share does not necessarily imply high market power. The chief criticism of the theory is that it loses force if the incumbent can cut price quickly. If that is the case, then it need not price competitively before entry. In spite of the strong claim made by William Baumol and other advocates, the majority of researchers who study industrial organizations are of the opinion that empirical evidence does not provide support for the hypothesis that potential entry is at least as important as actual entry as a constraint on market power. The airlines industry in the USA has not proved to be contestable after deregulation in 1978.

BOX 3.1: Airlines Deregulation in the USA

The number of carriers rose from thirty-three in 1976 to ninety-eight in 1982 and existing carriers extended their networks. Despite higher fuel costs, fares per mile declined by an average of 8.5 per cent, particularly on long hauls and flights between large cities. New entrants had advantage of non-union labour. Wages of airlines employees experienced a sharp drop. Passengers did not show any reluctance to accept the lower quality–lower price package offered by the majority of newcomers. Things moved in nice accord with contestability theory for a while, but by the late 1980s many new entrants had failed and industry concentration was on the rise. One observer commented, 'The easiest way to become a millionaire is to start as a billionaire and invest in the airlines business'. This was chiefly due to the actions of the major airlines who used essential facilities (hub-and- spoke networks centred on major airports) and control of computer reservation systems to drive out rivals. The experience of the USA, and also of the UK where domestic routes were substantially deregulated in the 1980s, shows that after an initial bout of welfare enhancing competition the industry tends to settle back into oligopoly.

Source: Vickers and Yarrow (1998).

Apart from X-inefficiency and allocative inefficiency caused by P > MC, monopoly power is at the root of one more welfare reducing phenomenon known as rent seeking. Whenever supernormal profit persists in any activity agents will expend resources to capture or perpetuate it. This is pure waste from the social point of view. Since the value of resources spent will vary directly with the value of monopoly profit in the targeted industry (the prize), some economists are in favour of ignoring the entire producers' surplus while calculating the social benefit of monopoly. That is, they would add area B to area C to arrive at the welfare loss relative to the competitive optimum. Although this may be a bit too harsh, the kernel of truth in the idea cannot be denied.

One group of economists, the Austrian school, maintains that the standard criticism of monopoly in terms of allocative inefficiency (P > MC) is fundamentally flawed because it ignores dynamic efficiency, which refers to the introduction of new and better products as well as innovations leading to technological progress. Monopoly, according to this view, has greater capacity for dynamic efficiency than a perfectly competitive system composed of numerous atomistic firms. The Austrian economist, Joseph Schumpeter, put it like this:

> As soon as we go into the details and inquire into the individual items in which progress was most conspicuous, the trail leads not to the doors of those firms that work under conditions of comparatively free competition but precisely to the doors of the large concerns.

Perfect competition, therefore, 'has no title to being set up as a model of ideal efficiency'.

The evils of monopoly may be summarized as: (a) allocative inefficiency, (b) X-inefficiency, and (c) rent seeking. To be set against this is dynamic efficiency.

MEASURING MARKET POWER

Market power is usually measured by two methods:

Elasticity of Demand

The price cost margin $(P - MC)/P$ (also called the Lerner index) is usually taken as a measure of market power or imperfection. But this can be shown to be just the reciprocal of the price elasticity of demand (at the profit maximizing point). This follows from $MR = MC$ and $MR = P(1 - 1/e)$.

The Lerner index makes intuitive sense because the larger the number of sellers the higher an individual firms' price elasticity is likely to be. At one extreme, a perfectly competitive firm faces infinitely elastic demand so that the index takes the value zero. In oligopoly (of the Cournot type) the index becomes (s_i/e), where s_i is the market share of the ith firm (see Appendix).

Measures of Concentration

Concentration shows the extent to which the provision of a particular good or service is controlled by a few large sellers. It is usually measured using either concentration ratios, the Herfindahl index or the Gini coefficient.

The m-firm concentration ratio (C_m) is the share of the top m firms in an industry. The shares may be of sales, profits, assets, or employment. C_4 is the measure most widely used in empirical work. Thus C_4 = 0.6 means that 60 per cent of total industry sales (assuming a sales-based measure) is accounted for by the top four companies. Table 3.1 gives some illustrative C_4 values for different countries and industries for 1991.

Table 3.1: C_4 Values for Selected Countries and Industries

Industry	UK	US	Japan
Salt	99.5	82	41.5
Flour	94	46	67
Sugar	38	27	48
Beer	59	81	99.9
Pet food	83	64	39

Source: Sutton (1991).

One problem with C_m is that the distribution within the top m does not affect its value although such distribution may well make a difference to the effective degree of market power in the field. If $C_4 =$ 0.6 it could be because each of the top four has share of 15 per cent or because the first has 40 per cent and the other three a total of 20 per cent. Also, consider two industries A and B. In industry A the top company controls 70 per cent of the market and thirty companies have equal share of 1 per cent each. In industry B each of four top firms controls 20 per cent and there are twenty other firms each with a share of 1 per cent. Clearly industry B is more competitive, but has a higher C_4 value (80 as against 73). An alternative measure that uses the share of all firms in an industry is the Herfindahl index.

$$H = \Sigma s_i^2$$

H is the sum of squared shares of all firms. Sometimes the value of H is multiplied by 10,000 to get rid of the decimal. For the example given above:

Industry A: $H = (0.7)^2 + 30 (0.1)^2 = 0.493$

Industry B: $H = 4(0.2)^2 + 20 (0.1)^2 = 0.162$

So by this measure industry B is less concentrated or more competitive.

H takes the value 1 for monopoly. If there are n firms of equal size $s_i = 1/n$ and $H = 1/n$. For a competitive industry with a large number of identical firms H will be close to zero. (1/n tends to zero as n becomes larger and larger.)

It can be shown that in a Cournot oligopoly there is an exact relationship between price cost margin, the Herfindahl index, and the elasticity of demand. The relation is

$$(P - \bar{c}) / P = H / e$$

where $\bar{c} = \Sigma\ s_i c_i$ is the weighted sum of the (constant) MCs of the n firms, the weights being the market shares. Thus the degree of market imperfection indexed by the price cost margin is positively related to H and inversely related to e (see Appendix for proof).

The Herfindahl index is used as an instrument of industrial policy. The US Justice Department, for example, subjects to close scrutiny any merger proposal that will tend to push up H beyond certain specified limits. It had switched to H from the four firm concentration ratio after 1982.

Gini coefficient

It is based on the Lorenz Curve for a particular industry. Such a curve is shown in Figure 3.2.

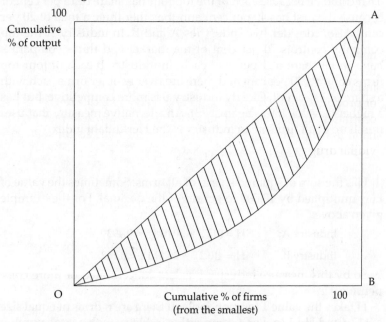

Figure 3.2: Lorenz Curve

The firms are ranked by size (output or employment or sales or assets) and cumulated from the lowest as a percentage of the total number of firms in the market. This is plotted on the horizontal axis against the cumulated share of size on the vertical. The diagonal is the line of absolute equality. The greater the divergence of the actual curve from the diagonal the greater the disparity in firm size. The Gini coefficient is the ratio of the shaded area to the triangle OAB. It varies between zero, when all the firms are of equal size (the Lorenz Curve coincides with the diagonal) and unity, when a single firm serves the market.

In an open economy where foreign competition is present in the form of exports and imports concentration measures based purely on domestic production and sales may not give a true picture of the degree of concentration and market power of domestic sellers. The following formula is often used to adjust concentration ratios for international trade:

$$C_m = Q_m - X_m / Q - X + M$$

where Q_m: sales at home and abroad by the m largest domestic firms
   X_m: exports by the m largest domestic firms
   Q, X, and M are total sales, total exports, and total imports respectively.

One serious problem that confronts the applied economist when he tries to calculate concentration measures is the distinction between the industry and the relevant market. Official data invariably relate to industries whereas he may be more interested in a particular product or product group. For example, a relatively moderate degree of concentration in the pharmaceutical industry as a whole may well go hand in hand with high concentration in the markets for some individual drugs.

PUBLIC POLICY IN IMPERFECTLY COMPETITIVE MARKETS

In the presence of monopoly power the state can intervene in many forms. In this section we take up the major ones—public provision, regulation, and promotion of competition.

Public Provision

The state nationalizes privately-owned firms and runs them to maximize social welfare. This involves bringing prices in line with marginal costs. Other decisions regarding investment in capacity, location of plants, product selection and so on are also taken keeping the public interest in mind. The opposite action of nationalization is privatization.

The primary disadvantage of public provision is that the discipline of the market being absent there is no effective check against inefficiency. The fear of bankruptcy does not exist because the government can always be counted on to bail out by infusing capital. That is, the manager faces what the Hungarian economist, Janos Kornai, has aptly termed a 'soft budget constraint'. Besides, it is not easy to judge what constitutes poor performance when profit is not an important objective. Low profit or loss, that is really caused by low productivity of labour and management, can always be blamed on socially worthwhile but commercially unprofitable policies. Thus, 'public interest' can be used as a smoke screen for the pursuit of private interests. This problem is known as that of 'moral hazard' in modern microeconomic theory. It occupies a prominent place in the general principal–agent problem.

An agency relationship exists whenever there is a service contract in which one person's welfare is directly affected by what another person does. The agent is the person who acts under the contract in exchange for remuneration and the principal is the person who employs the agent and is affected by his action. For example, in a business enterprise the managers and the workers are agents and the owners (shareholders) are the principal. A doctor is the agent of the patient and so on.

An agency relationship causes an agency problem to the detriment of efficiency when the parties involved have asymmetric information about some important aspects of the transaction. Two forms of asymmetry have received the most attention in the economics of information.

Adverse selection or hidden information

One party to a contract has more information about some relevant, exogenous factors than the other. For example, somebody purchasing life insurance knows much more about his own state of health than the insurance company, the seller of an old piece of machinery may know about some defect that the potential buyer is not aware of. This gives incentive for pre-contract opportunism.

Moral hazard or hidden action

In adverse selection one party has more information about some pertinent factor but he cannot do anything to influence that factor.

Hidden action refers to the case when, having entered a contract, the agent is able to take actions that can influence the outcome but cannot be fully observed by the principal. This unobservability (or costly monitoring) opens the door for post-contract opportunism.

In any modern economy shareholding in most large corporations is so dispersed that effective control lies with the management. Information gathering and monitoring by the owners or their representatives being costly, the manager can exercise considerable discretion to pursue his own goal at the cost of lower profit for the owners. Although there is no consensus in the literature on the objectives of managers, most views stress the value of high growth and large market share (empire building, more power) and more perks and fringe benefits.

The market, however, also contains some mechanisms to limit the managers' ability to deviate from the objectives of owners. If poor profit performance makes takeover more likely by depressing the share price, managers will suffer for not paying sufficient attention to profits. They face the prospect of being dismissed by the new owners. Market-based remuneration schemes such as stock options, stock appreciations rights, etc. link the managers' remuneration directly with shareholder's welfare. Also, if there is a developed managerial labour market it will induce managers to enhance their reputation (and market value) by running their firms efficiently. None of these devices (remuneration schemes, corporate takeover, and managerial labour market) can be relied on to work perfectly to completely eliminate the problem of moral hazard in private enterprises. Yet it is undeniable that they do succeed to a considerable extent in imposing discipline on managers and ensuring efficiency (or limiting inefficiency). (The managers themselves have come up with ingenious devices to blunt the edge of market discipline. These takeover defences are discussed in the Glossary.)

In public sector enterprises (PSEs) the agency problem is more serious because of their insulation from market discipline and the nebulous objective of pursuing public interest. The government intervenes directly in the decision-making of state-owned industries in order to attain wider social objectives and this provides management with an excuse for X-inefficiency and poor performance. Since performance itself is hard to measure in money terms given the social orientation, managers' financial remuneration cannot be clearly related to the performance of the firm. Monitoring of PSEs is done by bureaucrats who themselves face weak incentives and controls, so that it is easy for them to succumb to moral hazard and fail in their task of exposing poor management. Thus the agency problem proliferates throughout the system. It should, however, be pointed out that often it is bureaucratic bungling or political interference rather than moral hazard of managers that is chiefly responsible for the disappointing performance of PSEs.

The economic collapse of the centrally planned economies of the former Soviet bloc illustrates the havoc that unchecked agency problems can cause in organizations. Those economies were plagued and ultimately wrecked by the problem at three levels:

(a) Manager–worker: Worker motivation was low due to (i) no fear of jobloss (ii) little incentive to earn more as consumption goods and services were of bad quality and in short supply ('They pretend to pay us and we pretend to work'.)

(b) Planner–manager: Instead of fulfilling plans managers entered into bargaining relationship with planner–politicians. They had low motivation for efficiency.

(c) Public–planner: The communist party ceased to be an efficient agent of the public due to the absence of political competition.

When government failure is a possibility welfare comparison may go either way. Figure 3.1 shows that under private monopoly production stops before the social optimum Q_c has been reached. If, after government takeover, production is expanded all the way to the optimum the area C will be the net gain to society. Most unfortunately, other parameters may change to nullify this. Public officials may lack the initiative to minimize costs and as a result average and marginal cost may go up. If public sector managers are 'too inefficient', cost of the additional production may actually exceed the gain to consumers and the result of nationalization may be a decline in welfare.

Traditional welfare economics relied on a monolithic, benevolent government to address social problems. In sharp contrast, modern positive theory of government (public choice theory, pioneered by James Buchanan, Gordon Tullock among others) recognizes that a policy adopted by the state in any context is the result of complex interactions among politicians, bureaucrats, and managers and workers in PSEs, with each group striving to maximize its own private interest. It is extremely unlikely that the chosen policy will coincide with that required to achieve social optimality. This fundamental problem will not be solved even if information is freely available and policies can be costlessly implemented.

THE NATURAL MONOPOLY CASE AGAINST COMPETITION

A natural monopoly is said to exist when scale economies are so large, relative to the market size, that the market output is produced at least cost when there is only one firm. Monopoly is the natural and most efficient outcome. Competition will lead to needless duplication and wastage. The technology in this case features cost sub-additivity. Formally, the cost function C(q) is sub-additive if

$$C(q) \leqq C(q_1) + C(q_2) + \ldots + C(q_n)$$

where $q = \Sigma q_i$.

It is strictly sub-additive if the strict inequality holds. It can be proved that if there are increasing returns to scale throughout then cost function will be sub-additive, although the converse is not true. To show that sub-additivity does not imply increasing returns consider the cost function

$C(q) = F + cq$, where F is fixed cost and c is the constant value of MC. Take $q = q_1 + q_2$, so
$C(q_1) + C(q_2) = 2F + c(q_1+q_2) = F + C(q) > C(q)$.

So there is strict sub-additivity of cost, but constancy of MC rules out increasing returns.

Network industries (electricity, telecommunications, post, gas, railways, water, etc.) display cost sub-additivity. Welfare theory has traditionally prescribed state control of such sectors, either through state ownership or by regulation. Introduction of competition will cause inefficiency by raising the cost of producing any given output. John Stuart Mill observed in 1848:

It is obvious, for example, how great an economy of labour would be obtained if London were supplied by a single gas or water company instead of the existing plurality. Were there only one establishment, it would make lower charges consistently with the rate of profit now realised.

Lately, the classification of public utilities and other industries as natural monopolies has come to be seriously questioned because such industries often show cost sub-additivity only in certain parts of their activities. In electricity, for example, there is scale economy in distribution and having two parallel grid networks will be awfully wasteful. However, at the stage of generation, scale economy is much more limited. Similarly, in railways and telecommunications the natural monopolies will be the tracks and the local networks respectively. So, the proponents of liberalization argue, it should be possible and desirable to introduce competition in segments which are not subject to strong scale economies. In the USA, in 1984, AT&T was broken up into a series of regional telecom operators. The long distance market was opened to competition while monopoly was preserved (under regulation) in the local markets. However, this solution is not free from problems as we shall see in the section on regulation.

Sometimes it is claimed that there is no need for state control or regulation of a natural monopoly if the sector is contestable, because the threat of potential entry will eliminate monopoly power. As already noted, most economists, however, are sceptical about the importance of contestability in actual market situations.

Regulation

This involves monitoring the performance of firms that are in the private sector or have been moved there under denationalization or privatization. The primary objective is to bring their conduct closer to the social optimum by putting explicit checks on the exercise of monopoly power.

The simplest way to eliminate the allocative inefficiency of monopoly is to enforce marginal cost pricing. The monopoly will then operate at point T_2 instead of point T_1 in Figure 3.1. One problem with this solution is that it may imply negative profits for the firm.

Consider an industry that enjoys substantial economies of scale. Its averages as well as marginal costs, AC and MC, will be declining with output, and MC will be less than AC as AC is falling. In this case setting P = MC implies that price fails to cover average cost. This is shown in Figure 3.3.

Under MC pricing the firm operates at T_2 with P < AC, implying loss. Obviously, the situation cannot continue indefinitely. The usual solution was for the regulator to give a subsidy to the firm. But this subsidy does not come free of cost. If it is raised through taxation then the efficiency loss through that taxation has to be weighed against the efficiency loss from unregulated monopoly (which MC pricing was supposed to eliminate).

A more serious problem is that since the subsidy is a transfer from the regulator to the firm, it opens up the possibility of moral hazard on the part of the regulator. A mutually beneficial deal can be struck in which in exchange for a side payment the regulated agent obtains

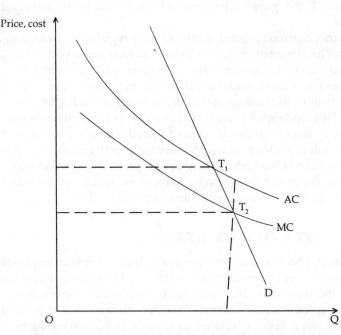

Figure 3.3: Average Cost Pricing under Increasing Returns

a hefty payment as subsidy. (Remember it is up to the regulator to fix the subsidy depending on the calculated gap between P and AC at the optimum output.) This is known as 'regulatory capture'. Numerous studies exist which document that in the USA and the UK regulation has favoured particular producer groups at the cost of wider national interest. In fact, economists of the Chicago school have argued that regulatory capture is so profitable that it is often the industry itself that lobbies for state control! It is also fairly common for politicians to select areas for regulation with an eye to their election prospects. Economic efficiency is often the last item on their priority list.

Transfer of public funds to any loss-making unit as subsidy has several negative consequences: (a) it encourages other firms to engage in subsidy seeking through lobbying; (b) it requires distortionary taxation elsewhere in the economy; and (c) there are transaction costs of transferring the subsidy. Thus, it usually costs the society more than Re 1 to transfer Re 1 to loss-making producers.

Given the problem with subsidies for falling cost industries, an alternative is average cost pricing. Here the firm, instructed to operate at T_1 in Figure 3.3, just breaks even. Production remains sub-optimal.

Another common practice is rate of return regulation, under which an upper limit is set on the return that a firm can earn on cost or capital invested during the current period. The major problem with this type of regulation is that it leads to cost inefficiency. There is an incentive for the firm to increase capital in order to achieve a higher level of profit. This tendency for overcapitalization ('padding the rate base') relative to least cost use of inputs in production is known as the Averch–Johnson effect. (see Appendix for proof). Once again, if the cost distortion is too high the original purpose of regulation may be defeated. Regulated firms also try to cheat on quality, which may be difficult to detect. Lower quality lowers social welfare.

DIRECT PRICE CONTROL (PRICE CAP)

Price regulation linked to average or marginal cost encourages ineffi-ciency, since any rise in costs will be covered by higher price permit-ted by the regulators. Managers have incentive to present padded expense accounts and welcome the opportunity to enjoy peace by allowing wage hikes unrelated to growth in labour productivity. There will also be reluctance to adopt cost-reducing innovations. AT&T in the USA was remarkably slow in introducing automated switching equipment.

Price cap is the mechanism which tries to avoid such problems by setting price beforehand so that incentive for cost reduction is maxi-mum. The standard formula (first popularized in the public utilities of the UK) is known as 'RPI minus X'. The price is permitted to rise each year over a specified period at the rate of inflation of the retail price index (RPI) minus a factor X per cent. The regulator sets X at the rate of expected cost reduction through improvement in productiv-ity. The X factor ensures that the benefits of productivity gain are enjoyed by the consumers. Price will be falling as long as the rate of inflation is less than X.

The formula is more difficult to operate when the firm has multiple products. Then a price index will have to be constructed with differ-ent weights for different commodities and the cap fixed in terms of this index. Capping individual products will be too unmanageable. But fixing an index cap leaves the firm with considerable scope to juggle about with the individual prices in the bundle.

The firm's incentive to invest in cost reduction will be dampened if success leads to a tightening of the cap in the next round. This is an example of the ratchet effect, which captures the tendency for performance standards to rise after a period of good performance. Thus, efficient managers of Soviet enterprises were 'punished' by having the production quota raised for the next quarter. Naturally, the managers were not too keen on improving performance through innovation. Therefore, to have the desired cost-efficiency effect price caps should be left untouched for several years, but the experience of the UK shows that if utilities start earning too high a rate of return intense political pressure builds up for lowering the cap because the time at which consumers benefit is delayed.

An example will support the point. British Telecom (BT) became a public limited company in April 1984 and was privatized in November that year. A price cap of RPI – 3 was chosen after negotiation between BT and the Department of Trade and Industry. Mercury Communications Limited was the sole competitor and no further competition was licensed until 1990. The price cap proved too generous owing to rapid technical advance and high growth of demand, enabling BT to earn handsome profits. This underscores a dilemma faced by the regulator—the tradeoff between allocative and dynamic efficiency. If the price cap is low relative to cost, return on investment is low, leading to inadequate capital investment in the industry and also a possible lowering of quality. On the other hand, a wide price cost margin confers monopoly power and creates allocative inefficiency.

Another serious problem emerges as the regulation period (interval of time over which the bound on price or return was set) draws to a close. It is now time for regulatory review and the firm is tempted to initiate actions to influence the outcome of the review. This strategic behaviour may lead to substantial squandering of valuable resources.

So far we have focussed almost exclusively on profitability regulations in the product market. Governments, however, may impose other restrictions as well (health and safety measures, for example) and may intervene in the factor market to prevent exploitation of labour.

An ingenious mechanism that promises to combine cost efficiency with allocative efficiency is known as yardstick competition. Tried in the water supply services in the UK, it is an application of the general proposition of incentive theory that it is optimal to make the reward of one agent partly contingent on the performance of others, when the chance factors facing them are strongly correlated. Regulated units are brought into competition with each other through regulation. Consider some firms in the same activity distributed geographically over regions A, B, and C. Price cap set in A may be made a function of cost performance in regions B and C. Provided that the firms operate in more or less similar environments and do not collude, this promises to deliver good results. Since the price faced by a producer is determined by the cost performance of other firms, it can keep for itself any gain from cost reduction and if the firms are from a similar industry price is kept in line with industry cost, which is good for allocative efficiency. Clearly, collusion among the firms will upset the scheme.

Optimal intervention in the market presumes that the regulatory authorities are in possession of enough information to identify the social optimum. MC pricing, for example, requires information about both demand and cost. Estimating MC for an enterprise is very hard not only for outsiders but often for insiders too. Much of the information needed has to come from the firm itself and the firm has every incentive to pass on false or distorted figures. Eliciting true and full information being either impossible or very expensive, too often the regulator has to work on the basis of a few crude indicators of performance such as return on book capital, rates of change in price, etc. While it may still be true that even imperfect regulation (provided the imperfection is not too severe) is better than no regulation from the point of view of public interest, greater awareness of the problems associated with regulation has enormously helped in putting the role of the state in a modern economy in proper perspective.

Just as private monopolies restrict output to enjoy greater profit, ill-designed or badly implemented government regulations also generate 'scarcity rents' by artificially creating rigidities and bottlenecks in the system. The beneficiaries of these institutional profits spend resources for their continuation. Through a business–bureaucrat–politician nexus (the 'iron triangle') even socially harmful regulations continue to be maintained and reinforced. For example, in Japan, the law requiring compulsory checking of cars for gas emissions and other mechanical troubles by authorized garages served a socially useful purpose in the days when Japanese cars and roads were of relatively poor quality. Now this type of control is no longer needed, but vested interest of garage owners has ensured its continuation. Encouragement of socially unproductive or harmful rent seeking activities is an important manifestation of government failure. Examples from the Indian experience can be multiplied at will.

Regulation of financial industries (which mobilize the savings of citizens) is justified on prudential grounds because of the high social cost of instability. Most governments do not allow market forces to have free sway in such industries with significant exit costs. For example, life insurance or life savings of pensioners. Similarly, too much competition among sellers in activities where the safety factor is important could lead to undesirable compromise on safety for the sake of cost reduction.

Globalization has introduced a new dimension to regulation. A tight regulatory regime may encourage MNCs to shift their production to other countries. Actually, as already noted in Chapter 2, the degree of regulatory control has become a strategy in the competition among nations to attract direct foreign investment (DFI). No country, especially a less developed one, which is counting heavily on such investment to pull it out of stagnation, will agree to a unilateral tightening of environmental or labour standards.

THE INTERCONNECTIONS PROBLEM

Advocates of deregulation of natural monopolies rightly want to introduce competition in those segments where scale economy is not an issue. The interconnections problem arises because these parts cannot be operational without the part that is a natural monopoly. Electricity generators need the distribution network, long distance carriers cannot do without the local network, competing airlines need the airport and so on. The money that the downstream competitors have to pay to the incumbent owning the essential capital or facility (the upstream firm) is the access fee. Determining the optimum level of the fee is a crucial step in the deregulation process. The issue is often complicated by the fact that the upstream firm itself is a competitor in the downstream market. For example, France Telecom owns the essential capital and also operates in the long distance market.

Privatization of the electrical power industry in Chile supplies an example of the type of problem that can arise if an investor is allowed to take control of an essential facility. After privatization the control of ENDESA, the major generating utility, passed to ENERSIS which owns the most important electricity distribution grid of the country. This created an almost insurmountable barrier to potential entrants into the market. It was left to competition law to compel ENDESA to deal with rivals on reasonable terms.

When telecommunication was deregulated in Germany, Deutsche

Telekom initially set the access fee at 6.5 pfennig per minute. This was much higher than the one-pfennig rate the competitors wanted. The regulator settled for 2.7 pfennig, the average for ten countries. This value was too low. There was a rush of entry and Deutsche Telekom lost a substantial share of the long distance business within a very short time. In December 1998 the access fee was raised.

A formula for setting the access fee that is widely used is the efficient component pricing rule (ECPR). It states that the price charged to a downstream competitor cannot exceed the difference between the price charged by the upstream firm in that segment and its MC at that stage. Suppose a telephone company C also operates in the mobile phone segment. Its price is P_1 and MC is c_2. There is another mobile phone company M with its own MC of c_2. Under ECPR the maximum fee that C can charge for the use of its essential capital is ($P_1 - c_1$). Let it be denoted by f. Then if M charges P_2 for its service the profit margin is

$$P_2 - (c_2 + f) = P_2 - (c_2 + P_1 - c_1) = (P_2 - P_1) + (c_1 - c_2)$$

The basic idea is that if M charges a competitive price ($P_2 = P_1$) then it can earn a profit only if it is more efficient ($c_2 < c_1$). Thus ECPR is supposed to promote efficiency. This, however, is at best partially true because there is no check in the rule on the monopoly power of the upstream firm (company C). The access fee has no relation with the cost of providing access. In the early 1990s a rival operator Clear Communications challenged the Telecom Corporation of New Zealand in court for charging an access fee that was too high and designed to drive it out of business. TCNZ won the case because it was following ECPR.

Apart from natural monopoly based on cost sub-additivity, another case justifying a certain level of market concentration for economic viability occurs when the magnitude of sunk costs in a venture as well as the degree of risk involved are too high. Development of jet engines and advanced microchips, for example, involve 'bet the company' risks, which may not be worth taking at all without risk-sharing alliances between investors. The special nature of the activity involved, it may be argued, calls for lenient treatment of such alliances by regulatory authorities.

Competition Policy

Preceding sections have dealt with existing monopoly power. But there is also need for vigilance against effort by firms to acquire or

---

BOX 3.2: BOT in Power Generation in the Philippines

In the Philippines the state-owned monopoly The National Power Corporation was in charge of generation and long distance transmission of power. Base load capacity was substantially below demand, power rates were very high and scheduled eight-hour power cuts were common.

In 1991 a build-operate-transfer (BOT) programme was introduced to boost investment in base load generating capacity. Natural monopoly of long distance distribution was separated from the power generating function. Even in power generation there were substantial scale economies relative to market size. Tenders were invited for the larger plants. Given the urgency of the situation small gas turbine projects were allowed to operate because they could be implemented quickly. Quotations were invited for the cost of electricity to be delivered to the transmission system. A precise analytical model was used by the government to calculate the return on investment on these projects as a function of operating costs and the length of the operate phase of the BOT. Most of the contracts negotiated were in the 25-year range.

Prices were in the range 1.80–1.90 pesos per kilowatt hour for small gas turbine projects. Subsequently a 1200 megawatt project was negotiated with Korea Electric Power with cost of 0.78 peso per kilowatt hour.

Over time, the power situation improved markedly, small gas turbines were replaced by larger coal-fired projects and with a decline in the risk factor cost of borrowing for the projects came down appreciably.

Source: World Investment Reports, various issues.

create such power. Anticompetitive practices are those undertaken by firms, jointly or in isolation, to restrict, distort, or prevent competition. Mergers, erection of entry barriers, predatory or discriminatory pricing are examples. Unless this type of conduct is checked by suitable policy, liberalization may be quite ineffective from the welfare point of view.

Mergers and acquisitions (M&A)

A merger of two or more firms takes place usually through an exchange of shares of the merging firms with shares of the new legal entity, which usually reflects the names of all the companies concerned (for example, Smith Kline Beecham or Ciba Geigy).

BOX 3.3: Major Restrictive Business Practices Addressed by
Competition Policy

Horizontal restraints

Price fixing	sellers enter into cooperative agreements regarding prices and sales conditions
Restraint of output	sellers enter into agreements regarding output and product quality
Market allocation	sellers allocate markets among themselves, depriving consumers of the benefits of competition
Exclusionary practices	sellers employ strategies that inhibit the ability of other actual or potential suppliers to compete in the market
Collusive tendering (bid rigging)	competing suppliers exchange sensitive information on bids and agree on who will submit the most competitive offer
Other restraints on competition	sellers enter into agreement not to undertake certain actions of competitive value (advertising, for example)

Vertical restraints

Exclusive dealing	a producer supplies particular distributors and guarantees not to supply other distributors in a given region
Reciprocal exclusivity	a producer supplies on the condition that the distributor does not carry products of another supplier
Refusal to deal	a seller refuses to sell to parties willing to buy
Resale price maintenance	a producer supplies distributors only on condition that the distributor sells at a minimum price set by the producer
Territorial restraint	a supplier sells to distributors only on the condition that the distributor does not sell the product outside a specified territory
Premium offers (loyalty rebates)	a supplier offers inducements only to certain parties on the condition they do not sell products of another supplier
Discriminatory pricing	different parties in similar circumstances are charged different prices

Tied selling	producer forces purchasers to buy goods they do not want as condition to sell them those that they want, or forces distributors to hold more goods than they wish
Predatory pricing	supplier sells at price below cost to drive competitors out of business
Full line forcing	a supplier requires distributors, for access to any product, to carry all of his products

A takeover (or acquisition) takes place when the management of one firm makes a direct offer to the shareholders of another and acquires a controlling interest (for example, Coca Cola's takeover of Parle India).

There are three major types of merger:

Horizontal: Firms producing similar goods and services (at the same stage of production) combine. Examples, Ford's takeover of Jaguar in automobiles, Glaxo merging with Wellcome in pharmaceuticals.

Vertical: Firms combine at different stages of production of the same good or services. This may be backward when a firm merges with a firm supplying inputs to it, or forward towards downstream activities, closer to the retail outlet. Major oil companies owning their own oil fields, refineries, and distribution networks provide a good example of both backward and forward integration.

Conglomerate: Firms in diverse lines of business are brought under the umbrella of a single company. Mitsubishi, the giant Japanese company with interest in cars, finance, and other activities, is a good example. The chaebols of South Korea also fall in this category.

M&As increase concentration in an industry by reducing the number of firms and also lead to a rise in profitability reflected in a wider price-cost margin. So, apparently, mergers reduce welfare by raising the degree of monopoly in a market. Government intervention is deemed necessary to counter the adverse effect. However, this view obscures the important fact that mergers frequently lead to a reduction in costs. This happens because of economies of scale at two levels. At the plant level there are the purely technical gains associated with specialization, dovetailing of processes and similar effects. Added to this are the firm-level economies leading to sharp reduction in the cost of administration, sales promotion, research and development, etc. Then there is the synergy effect of merger (the so-called '2+2 > 4' effect), whereby the efficiency of the combined firm rises by more than the sum of its parts. Economy of scope plays an essential role (see Glossary). This cost efficiency creates a dilemma for the regulator. In judging whether or not a proposed merger is in the public interest he has to set the likely cost savings against the rise in concentration. One study concluded that if monopoly leads to a reduction of average costs in the order of 5–10 per cent, the merger must lead to price increases in excess of 20 per cent (if price elasticity is 0.2) and in excess of 40 per cent (with elasticity of 0.05) for the net impact to be negative. Arriving at an unbiased estimate of the cost saving involved is very difficult, however, because the information lies with the merging firms themselves. Estimating the price effect is also problematic. One line is to calculate the effect of the merger on the Herfindahl index H and use the formula $(P - \bar{c})/ P = H/e$ (see Appendix).

Three general rules are usually followed in formulating public policy towards merger in most industrial economies: (a) the greater the induced price rise the larger is the welfare loss; (b) the smaller the market shares of the merging firms the lower is the welfare loss; (c) merger is less harmful in industries where entry is easy, because in such cases the price effect will not be very significant.

Globalization has given rise to the problem of transnational mergers. Consider two firms which are based in country A, but sell most of their output in country B. If they decide to merge and thereby acquire dominant position in B's market, higher profits will be realized in A but the loss in consumers' welfare will be confined to B. Under the circumstances getting the merger approved by the regulatory authority of country A may be fairly easy. But country B is entitled to object to this merger. Conceptually, this case is not different from any case of discriminatory trade policy. In a different type of case, the European Commission in 1991 prohibited the acquisition of de Havelland, a Canada-based aircraft producer by a European joint venture, ATR, on the ground that the merged entity will have excessive market power in Europe. The Canadian authorities did not oppose the merger. The merger between Boeing and McDonnel Douglas led to a confrontation between the USA and EU competition authorities that was finally resolved when Boeing gave an undertaking to restrict its use of long term exclusive contracts with major airlines. Clearly, there is much scope for improving international cooperation in competition law enforcement.

BOX 3.4: Competition Policy in Action

- The proposed acquisition by two companies, one from South Africa and one from the UK, of the company Impala Platinum Holdings Limited was blocked by the European Commission, because the move would have created a duopoly structure in the world platinum and rhodium market.
- The acquisition by Gillette of Braun, a major European producer of electric razors, was challenged by the USA on the ground that Gillette would enjoy substantially enhanced market power. A consent decree forced the company to divest the right to sell Braun razors in the USA to a newly created corporation.
- The US Department of Justice built up its case against Microsoft Corporation around the following alleged anticompetitive practices:

Predatory contracts: Microsoft often wrote contracts with hardware manufacturers that made it very unprofitable for them to install operating systems offered by rivals.

Deliberate incompatibility: Various tricks were used to create the false impression that DR–DOS (offered by Digital Research) will not work with Windows 3.1.

Vapourware: New products were repeatedly announced long before they were actually ready.

Bundling: Microsoft bundled its operating system with its own internet browser to keep out the rival browser software Netscape.

Source: World Investment Reports, The New Yorker (January 1998).

In enforcement of competition law the current trend reveals a preference for 'rule of reason' standard, under which no business practice is deemed legal or illegal by itself. Rather, legality is determined by the merits of the particular case concerned. This has improved flexibility in policy-making. At the same time, however, a rule of reason standard increases the risk of arbitrariness in decision-making and enhances the prospect of corruption. The more discretion the policy-makers have the greater the incentive to lobby.

TAKEOVERS IN INDIA

Under the Monopolies and Restrictive Trade Practices (MRTP) Act of 1969, there were numerous barriers to mergers, acquisitions, and takeovers. Bank financing of takeovers were not permitted by the Reserve Bank of India (RBI). Moreover, the board of a company had the power to refuse transfer to a particular buyer on two grounds—the transfer would hurt the interest of the company and/or the public interest. As a result, even grossly mismanaged firms did not have to fear any change of management.

In 1991 the MRTP (Amendment) Act was passed. The need for prior approval of the Central Government for M&A activities was abolished. As the number of mergers and acquisitions began to grow, the Securities and Exchange Board of India (SEBI), through the Substantial Acquisitions of Shares and Takeovers Regulations of 1994, sought to bring about a climate in which the capital market could more effectively fulfill its disciplining function against non-performing firms. One key element was to enforce greater transparency in the process through a carefully designed system of disclosure of information for both open market as well as negotiated takeovers.

The Bhagwati Committee, set up to review the regulations and recommend change, submitted its draft takeover code in August 1996. The avowed aim was to make the process of takeover smoother, more transparent, and more effective, without compromising the interests of shareholders and the principles of equity and fairness. Because the Committee recommended abolition of the existing condition of 20 per cent public holding after the offer acquirers now can make a company private. They have the option of buying out the remaining shares if the public holding falls short of 10 per cent subsequent to a public offer. Another important recommendation is that an acquirer must deposit 10 per cent of the total offer amount in an escrow account, which will be forfeited in the event of default by the acquirer.

COLLUSION

In simple terms collusion is a conspiracy of sellers against buyers. This is a very common phenomenon on which Adam Smith made a very famous remark in his classic, *The Wealth of Nations*: 'People of the same trade seldom meet together, even for merriment and diversion, but the conversation ends in a conspiracy against the public, or in some contrivance to raise prices'.

It can be shown that in an oligopoly the aggregate output will be higher than the monopoly output, price will be lower and the joint profit of the firms will fall short of the monopoly profit (see Appendix). As a result the sellers have a strong incentive to cut production, raise price, and share the monopoly profit among themselves. A cartel is a group of sellers who act under agreement to maximize joint profits. The sharp increase in oil prices engineered by the Organization of Petroleum Exporting Countries (OPEC) in 1973 is a classic example of cartel in action. The De Beers Corporation is another highly successful cartel in the diamond business.

However, collusive arrangements are difficult to sustain. This problem (known as the problem of cartel stability) is principally due to cheating or 'chiselling' by individual cartel members. Once the cartel is formed and the production quota set for the members, each firm will have a strong incentive to cheat on others by undercutting the price and selling more secretly. There will be no noticeable effect on the monopoly price if only one firm cheats, but since the same temptation works for everybody, all members will try to produce and sell in excess of their quotas and as a result price will crash. The agreement will come to a premature end.

A simple example will illustrate this result. Suppose that in a Cournot duopoly the market demand is given by $P = 8 - (q_1 + q_2)$ where q_1, q_2 are the outputs of the two firms. Each firm has constant $MC = 4$ and there is no fixed cost.

1. The monopoly solution obtained by maximizing profit $\pi_m = Pq - cq = (8-q) q - 4q$ yields $P = 6$ and $q = 2$. Total profit is 4. Since the firms are identical the cartel may be assumed to set $q_1 = q_2 = 2$. The sellers agree to charge a price of 6 in the market and share the profit of 4 equally.

2. If firm 2 cheats by charging 5 while firm 1 is charging 6 as per agreement, firm 2 grabs the entire market. Since $q_1 = 0$, $q_2 = 8 - 5 = 3$, firm 1's profit is zero, while 2 enjoys profit of 5 (3) – 4(3) = 3.

3. By symmetry, if firm 1 cheats and firm 2 honours the agreement, 2 earns zero, while 1 gets 3.

4. If both firms cheat and charge 5, total market demand will be 3. Assuming that each gets half the customers, each produces 1.5 units and earns profit of 5 (1.5) – 4 (1.5) = 1.5.

The payoff (profit) matrix is given below (the first number in each cell is firm 1's profit):

		Firm 2	
		Agreement (Rs 6)	Cheating (Rs 5)
Firm 1	Agreement (Rs 6)	(2, 2)	(0, 3)
	Cheating (Rs 5)	(3, 0)	(1.5, 1.5)

If firm 1 sticks to the agreement, it is better for firm 2 to break it because it can thereby raise its profit from 2 to 3. If firm 1 cheats, it is still better for firm 2 to cheat because otherwise its profit will fall to zero. So, no matter what its partner does, cheating remains the best strategy for firm 2. It is the dominant strategy. By exactly similar logic, cheating is the dominant strategy of firm 1 also. So, following self interest, both cheat (charge Rs 5) and the agreement breaks down. (This is an example of what is known as Prisoners' Dilemma in game theory (see Glossary)). The firms end up in the lower right cell of the payoff matrix, each earning profit of 1.5. Sustained collusion would have placed them in the upper left cell with higher profit of 2 each.

The striking point is that although both firms are fully aware of the gains from cooperation (the payoff matrix is fully known) they have no way of entering an agreement that will be proof against opportunistic behaviour. But collusion may be maintained by very subtle strategies that will modify the structure of payoffs, as will be shown later.

The cartel instability problem shows clearly that the success of a collusive agreement will depend crucially on the difficulty of detecting cheating and punishing the guilty. The members will have to have some mechanism for monitoring their own activities. The economic power will generally not be equally distributed across the cartel members and the task of monitoring may be expected to be taken up by the dominant player. Thus Saudi Arabia acted as OPEC's 'policeman' for a long time. It is not hard to see that collusion will be easier to sustain if the sellers are not too heterogeneous, their number is small, and the product is homogeneous. Also, the industry should not be subject to random shocks because in that case it may be difficult to negotiate and to figure out whether changes in productions are really due to deliberate deviation from the agreed-upon quota. If the product is not homogeneous then secret price concessions may be given by changing some qualitative attribute that is not easily observable.

Profit from successful collusion is so high that in numerous industries firms have found out ways of sustaining the cooperative solution through appropriate monitoring, punishment, and other ingenious strategies. One such strategy, the 'most favoured customer clause', is discussed later. It should also be noted that collusion may not be restricted to price fixing alone. It may involve other types of agreements as well, like setting the level of product quality or not invading each other's territory. The chemical industry in the 1920s had an agreement by which it was decided that Dupont would concentrate

BOX 3.5: OPEC and the Price of Oil

When a glut in the market brought down sharply the international price of oil in 1960, five producers decided to form a cartel—the Organization of Petroleum Exporting Countries. Throughout the 1960s it became stronger and stronger and membership grew from five to thirteen. By 1977 OPEC's shares in the global stock of oil and production were one-half and two-thirds respectively. Between 1973 and 1974 OPEC was able to effect a four-fold rise in price. This is the first 'oil shock' that had such a profound impact on the world economy. This is shown in the Table B3.5.1.

Table B3.5.1: Price of Crude Oil (US$ per barrel)

				First shock			Second shock		Collapse	
Year	1960	1969	1971	1973	1974	1977	1980	1985	1986	1989
Price	1.91	1.51	2.49	3.03	11.65	13.66	28.0	30.0	15.0	14.4

In 1979 the revolution in Iran disrupted supply from that country and OPEC was again able to raise price drastically (the second 'oil shock'). Over time, however, its power has been considerably eroded owing to conservation measures and emergence of rival suppliers. The share of non-OPEC producers in total supply went up from 47 per cent in 1973 to 69 per cent in 1986. (After the June 1996 meeting of OPEC oil ministers a press release said, 'The conference also served notice on non-OPEC producers that it is in the common interest of both sides to work towards improving the price. The ministers urged non–OPEC producers to exercise production restraint'.) Currently the price is around US$ 25 per barrel, while unit cost is approximately US$ 8.

Source: Ethier (1995).

on the USA; German firms on Europe, and ICI on the UK and the Commonwealth countries. Although this was subsequently declared illegal, without doubt similar agreements are still in operation all over the world.

Though the need for public policy to fight collusion is clear and beyond question, implementation of such policy runs into serious practical difficulties. There is no simple test of tacit collusion. The only workable rule seems to be that collusion can be inferred if an industry with high concentration is able to sustain supernormal profits over a long period. But calculation of such profits is far from easy or reliable, particularly as figures relating to sales and costs have to come from the firms themselves.

It is also possible for cartel arrangements to evade the machinery of law enforcement by taking on the disguise of legal agreements. For example, a perfectly legal agreement among firms to restrict the emission of pollutants may really be just a device for restricting aggregate output. Practices such as these make life extremely hard for antitrust authorities.

Sellers often maintain collusion by ingenious and hard-to-penetrate strategies. The 'most favoured customer' clause is an example. It binds a firm not to offer a discount to a particular customer without offering the same to every other customer within a specified period. By making price cutting costly such an offer helps to sustain a high price.

Consider a market with two sellers A and B. Each has only two price quotations, high (H) and low (L). The payoffs are given below (the first number in each cell is A's profit)

		B's price	
		H	L
A's price	H	(100,100)	(0, 130)
	L	(130, 0)	(70, 70)

For each firm, charging L gives a higher profit regardless of what the other charges. (L is a dominant strategy). So the outcome is the choice of L by both and each ends up earning profit of 70. The collusive solution (H, H) cannot be sustained as it pays to break the agreement by charging L.

Now suppose the firms introduce a price guarantee to purchasers in the form of a 'most favoured customer' clause. If price is ever reduced, earlier customers will get a rebate. This reduces the attraction of changing from H to L. A price cut brings in new buyers but also entails the penalty of refunding previous customers. The new payoff matrix is:

		B's price	
		H	L
A's price	H	(100,100)	(0, 90)
	L	(90, 0)	(70, 70)

Now if both firms start by choosing H neither has any reason to deviate. So collusion can be maintained. A clause that apparently protects the consumer really serves the sellers' interest.

Another paradoxical result is that government regulations aimed at improving transparency in market transactions may actually harm the consumer. This is because if prices are made public, offering secret price discounts to customers becomes impossible and the main threat to collusion (chiselling) is removed. This was dramatically illustrated by the sharp rise in the average price in the oligopolistic ready-mixed-concrete industry in Denmark after the government had decided in 1993 to gather and publish regularly the transaction prices of the major firms. Transparency actually strengthened market power at the cost of consumers. The decision was ultimately revoked.

Many developed countries including the USA, France, Germany, the UK, and Japan have legal provisions for the operation of export cartels targeting foreign markets. They are allowed because there is no adverse impact on the competitive environment in the domestic economy. One notable case was that of the European wood pulp in which the European Commission decreed in 1984 that forty producers of wood pulp located in the USA, Canada, Finland, Norway, Portugal, Spain, and some of their affiliates were guilty of restricting price competition within the EU and had hindered free trade between its member states during 1973–81.The most interesting feature is that none of the producers in the export cartel were located within the Union at that time. The Commission invoked the 'effects doctrine' to claim extraterritorial jurisdiction. This underscores the need for international cooperation in enforcement of competition law. Such cooperation is often hampered by the use of 'blocking statute' by countries that bars firms from disclosing information to foreigners. Competition authorities often tolerate the formation of cartels in industries that are struggling against rising imports. The EU has permitted, indeed promoted, a number of such recession cartels in recent years.

PREDATORY PRICING AND STRATEGIC ENTRY DETERRENCE

Business practices aimed primarily at forcing rivals out of business are known as predation. Its usual form is the setting of low prices, sustaining losses in the short run, in order to gain more profit eventually by eliminating competition. In the context of international trade this is known as dumping (see Chapter 6).

Here is an example of predatory behaviour. The Netherlands-based multinational AKZO had a 50 per cent share of the European market for a particular type of chemical additive. In the UK its share was high but it faced serious competition from a small local firm ECS. When ECS decided to enter the German market for the additive, AKZO issued a threat that unless it withdrew immediately it would retaliate in the UK by 'going below cost, if necessary'. ECS applied for and obtained an injunction against the giant MNC. The case continued and eventually AKZO had to pay a hefty fine.

There is a view associated with the economists of Chicago that in the absence of barriers to takeover, predatory pricing should not exist because the predator would save time and effort by simply buying up the competitor. But strong empirical evidence exists to indicate that predation does take place on a significant scale. However, identifying predatory action is difficult because price cut by an incumbent following new entry may well be a competitive response to entry, a perfectly legitimate and indeed welcome move. As with collusion, there is no simple test of predation. The most widely used criterion is that any price below average variable cost or marginal cost is predatory, while price above average total cost is not. While relatively easy to apply for single product firms, the test may be rendered ineffective by multiproduct monopolies who can manipulate the allocation of joint costs among products. Post-exit price rise is a robust indicator of predation, but it cannot be used to judge cases where predation is going on but the objective of the rival's exit is yet to be achieved.

The test mentioned above rightly rejects average total cost as a reference point, because there are many instances where a seller is forced to sell below average cost as a normal business practice. In times of declining or depressed demand, setting price below average total cost but above average variable cost is perfectly legitimate because it enables the firm to recover its variable costs plus a portion of the fixed costs. The loss is lower than what it would be if the firm stopped production (in which case loss will equal its full fixed cost). In some other cases too below-marginal cost or below-average cost pricing may be normal strategies that have nothing to do with predation. An experience good is one whose quality can be ascertained only upon actual consumption. Consumers typically pay more for their subsequent purchases of such goods than for their first purchase. To induce them to sample his good for the first time a seller may initially set price below cost. Also, when sellers are experimenting with new technologies or new products and enter the market for the first time their unit cost may well be above the sale price (a new product is by definition an experience good). Costs gradually come down through learning by doing (see Learning Curve in Glossary). In either case, below cost pricing cannot be viewed as predatory. In fact, it may be argued that it enhances productive efficiency, competition, and consumers' satisfaction. This would be the view of the Austrian school.

Strategic entry deterrence is an anticompetitive practice where an incumbent seller protects its market power by acting so as to make entry unprofitable to new firms. It threatens to respond to entry in such an aggressive way that the potential entrant backs out. The key condition is that the threat must be credible to be effective. It will be empty if it is not in the interest of the incumbent to carry it out when entry actually occurs. The incumbent must commit himself to a course of action that is not easily reversible and that would be sufficiently detrimental to the potential entrant. Installed capacity can be an effective deterrent, because it can be used to flood the market and bring down the price sharply once entry takes place. The incumbent will suffer temporary losses no doubt, but on the reasonable assumption that his staying power exceeds that of the newcomer, he will be the ultimate winner. His threat to use the capacity is credible because the cost of installing it has already been sunk. From the social point of view this strategic capital investment is undesirable, because its primary purpose is to thwart potential competition and not to meet current or projected demand in a cost efficient manner.

Pre-emptive patenting is another instrument of entry prevention. The incumbent acquires a patent with the sole purpose of denying a potential entrant access to technology that will enable him to compete. Here we have an explanation of the commonly observed phenomenon of patents not in active use by the right holder (sleeping or non-working patents).

Since strategic entry deterrence preserves monopoly power by undermining the freedom of entry into an industry, active policies are required to put a curb on this sort of behaviour.

FRANCHISE

It may be possible to retain state ownership or control while promoting competition by franchise or competitive tender. This is competition for the field, rather than in the field. In many countries including

India economic reform has involved franchising to introduce competition into the areas of health care, telecommunications, transport, etc. and other government activities such as construction under the public works department. Since 1988 public transport (both bus and train) has been subject to competitive bidding in Sweden. Japan invites competitive tender for train services along designated lines, so does the UK for long distance coach service on road.

The usual method is to award the franchise to the highest bidder. The most efficient firm should be able to bid the highest because it has the greatest profit potential. Another alternative is to offer the franchise to the firm that charges customers the lowest price for the service (subject to minimum quality standards). If there are a large number of bidders the result will be a price close to average cost, a large gain for consumers. The method has worked successfully for TV franchising in both the USA and the UK. The chief problem is that there is ample scope for post-contract opportunism, particularly in respect of quality, which may be hard to detect.

Since the franchisee has to bid again when the contract period expires he does not have much incentive for substantial capital investments that need time to bear fruit. The franchise period should be sufficiently long to enable him to reap the return of such investments and other cost saving innovations. But if it is too long the old problems associated with lack of competition will tend to return. Further, at the time of rebidding the current operator with inside knowledge and experience will be at an advantage. The implications for efficiency may not be good if the same party keeps on winning the contract time after time.

Franchising has been on the whole more popular in the USA than in Europe. The EU's competition policy tries to put curbs on the franchisor's control over the franchisee's operations. McDonald's, for example, cannot make its European franchisees sell only Coca Cola in preference to other brands.

PRIVATIZATION

The term 'privatization' is sometimes used in a broad sense, embracing not only change of ownership from the state to private agents but also relaxation of regulatory controls and general attempt to expose more economic activities to the pressures of market forces (deregulation or liberalization). In this chapter we shall use it in the narrow sense of ownership transfer.

Does Ownership Matter?

Although most mainstream economists and the majority of the general public hold that PSEs are less profitable and less efficient than private business corporations, several studies tend to confirm that the crucial element is the degree of competition prevailing in the sphere where the unit operates. That is, a PSE is not inherently inefficient; a private firm sheltered from competition may display exactly the same kind of inefficiency. A lax system of incentives or control may cause a PSE to perform worse than its private sector counterpart, but this may not be true of a state firm operating within a tighter and better designed set of rules. The fact that contracting out through competitive tendering of services has led to substantial reduction in costs along with improvement in quality in numerous cases in Europe and the USA also lends support to the view that ownership transfer is not essential. The experience of successful reform in China also underscores the same conclusion. When China launched its programme of economic reform in 1979 the problem of inefficiency, corruption, and low worker and managerial motivation in the state enterprises had already assumed alarming proportions. The government retained full ownership but introduced several novel measures to boost productivity.

1. Managers were allowed to sell any output in excess of the production quota in the free market including foreign markets and to retain a substantial share of the profits made. They had more freedom to choose the mix of both products and inputs.
2. PSEs could hire labour on contract and such workers could be laid off unlike the regular employees. The 1980s witnessed a steady growth in contractual employment.
3. Performance linked bonus schemes for workers were thoroughly redesigned. Better incentives for managers raised the effectiveness with which bonuses were used to elicit greater work effort.
4. PSEs were exposed to greater competition from other state firms and new non-state firms. Subsidies were drastically reduced.
5. A System Reform Commission was set up to implement and evaluate the process of reform. It interacted regularly with PSEs without intervening directly into their functioning.

As a result of these measures performance improved remarkably within a short period. Total factor productivity (TFP) (see Glossary) for the industrial firms increased at an average annual rate of almost

5 per cent over the period 1980–90. Another index of success is the growing competitiveness of state controlled firms in the international market for a wide array of commodities. Thus China has demonstrated that incentive reform plus greater competition can improve matters without privatization.

BOX 3.6: Privatization in Japan

In 1985 and 1987 three major public corporations—Nippon Telegraph and Telephone (NTT), Japan National Railways (JNR), and Japan Tobacco (JT) were privatized. The primary objectives were to reduce deficit and improve efficiency.

NTT, founded in 1952 as a government company, was privatized in April 1985. Charges for telephone service actually came down and customer service improved. Although it remained the dominant firm in the industry, it was exposed to increasing competition over time and its profits declined substantially.

JNR was privatized in April 1987. Although its record was good in respect of speed, safety, and punctuality it was plagued by deficit (despite frequent fare increases), political interference, and labour trouble. It was broken up into six regional railway companies and one freight company. Its old debt was taken over by a new JNR Accounts Settlement Corporation, which also held shares of the new companies. These companies recorded high profits and have raised fares only a couple of times. New managerial flexibility led to diversification into travel related services. Labour was retrenched on a large scale. Within five years operating costs fell by more than 10 per cent and revenue per employee rose. Quality of service also improved, as revealed by passenger surveys. Investment in remote, unprofitable routes declined.

The former Japan Tobacco and Salt, a government monopoly, was renamed Japan Tobacco after privatization. At the same time import restrictions on tobacco were lifted and the wholesale business was opened to both domestic and foreign firms. However, JT retains monopoly over domestic production of tobacco products and is required to buy all tobacco leaf grown at home. Operating efficiency has improved and more attention is being paid to customer satisfaction.

Source: Dictionary of the Japanese Economy, MIT Press, Cambridge, MA. (1995).

Proponents of privatization counter by asserting that without full ownership transfer it is simply not possible to bring the PSE under the same degree of market pressure as is faced by its counterpart. Cost of inefficiency falls on a private firm principally in two forms: (i) its cost of capital will rise as financial intermediaries become reluctant to lend to it or lend on stiffer terms, (ii) it will be subject to takeover raids. Under state ownership both of these penalties fail to bite because the government (tax payers) will always be the ultimate underwriter of debt (the soft budget constraint problem) and there is no possibility of takeover. Insulated from the threat of dismissal, management and workers can continue to function in the same indolent, effort mini-mizing manner as before. Moreover, political interference is unlikely to cease if the state retains ownership or controlling interest. These factors explain why the World Bank is so dogmatic: 'ownership itself matters'. While reform can improve the performance of PSEs tempo-rarily as in the case of China, it is not sustainable over longer periods. Even in China close to 30 per cent of all PSEs still incur losses that absorb a sixth of the government's budgetary expenditures. Also, in the Bank's opinion, despite wide variation in performance within each group 'the median point on the private enterprise spectrum lies higher than the median point on the public enterprise spectrum'.

Even if the above view is correct the point remains that the greatest benefit from privatization is to be expected when change of owner-ship is combined with measures to strengthen competition. Most unfortunately, promotion of competition is often forgotten as it comes into direct conflict with the revenue maximizing objective of the government. Since a monopoly is worth more to investors, sales receipts will be maximized if the PSE is sold with monopoly rights intact. Critics point out that on the majority of occasions the state has attached primary importance to creating attractive share issues which will sell easily. Ideally, only the non-performing PSEs should be discarded by the state. But the logic of the market dictates otherwise and the enterprises put up for sale are usually the profitable ones. The policy of the Government of India has followed the same pattern. The recent privatization of the profit-making Bharat Aluminium Com-pany (BALCO) has met with stiff opposition. The welfare implica-tions are by no means clear if a public utility monopoly is converted intact into a private sector monopoly. Usually the private monopoly is put under regulatory control but, as we have seen earlier, regula-tion itself runs into a whole battery of problems. Still, from the con-sumers' point of view imperfect regulation may be better than no regulation. No dilemma, however, exists for an economist of the Austrian school, because to him the dynamic efficiency of profit-seeking entrepreneurs always outweighs the static allocative inefficiency of monopoly. Therefore privatization, preferably without regulation, is always desirable.

One major motivation for privatization has been the desire to reduce budgetary deficits or the public sector borrowing requirement (PSBR). Sale of assets or shares raises government revenue on one side while public expenditure under several heads fall after privatization on the other. The sales receipt, however, is a one-time gain whereas the state loses an entire stream of future returns following the sale of a (profitable) PSE. This should not matter if the sale price equals the present value of expected returns. Unfortunately, for a variety of reasons ranging from incorrect estimation of future returns to underhand deals, most privatization issues have tended to be underpriced, with the consequence that valuable national assets have been sold at giveaway prices. Up to 1994 electricity privatization in the UK raised some £6.5 billion while the assets involved had a conservatively estimated value of £28 billion. Another case involved the valuation of a company that had received a total of £2.9 billion of taxpayers' money at only £150 million and that also on condition that the state wrote off £1 billion of accumulated losses and infused a further £800 million. In East Germany the central privatization agency (Treuhand) handed over firms to West German investors for a single token Deutschemark.

The justification of privatization is weakest when externalities are significant. Government intervention (ownership being a special form) may have its own problems, but here the onus is really on the champions of free market to prove that the cost of government failure is indeed significantly higher than that of market failure. One consideration that is particularly of major concern to LDCs is that of retrenchment. In situation of high unemployment the social cost of employing one extra worker is lower than its private cost. But a private concern will take only the private cost into account in its decision to hire or fire. For labour surplus economies such as India the problem of overstaffing in the public sector should not be blown out of proportion. Indeed, there is no clear evidence that labour related problems are more responsible for the poor performance of PSEs than managerial incompetence or political interference. Labour has the disadvantage of greater visibility. Overstaffing is often used as an excuse by the management and bureaucracy to hide their own failure and moral hazard. Privatization in India should be subject to the proviso that employment be maintained even if this depresses the incentive of potential buyers.

Financing Privatization

In many developing countries programmes of privatization are hampered by constraints on financing. In one African country, for example, the value of PSEs put up for sale in the first round was about ten times the value of total funds available to the five major banks for acquisition financing. Some governments make matters worse by offering low risk, tax free bonds side by side with putting PSEs up for sale. Restrictions on foreign ownership also often acts as a severe constraint on financing options.

Brazil compelled financial intermediaries and other institutional investors to hold a part of their assets in the form of 'privatization certificates'. Insurance companies and pension funds rightly objected by saying that such forced acquisition ran counter to regulations that forbade them to invest in high risk ventures. Mexico favoured outright sale for cash because that cleanly severs the troublesome umbilical cord between the enterprise and the state. Under this mode unpaid balances cannot be utilized to blackmail the state for further concessions, thereby eliminating any possibility of future hold up.

Selling for hard cash, however, may not be feasible for most LDCs. Then the government has to sell for debt. Such transactions involve a high degree of risk. In Latin America during the 1970s and 1980s failure of a large number of privatized firms was mainly due to highly leveraged (debt financed) sales. There was widespread bankruptcy and many PSEs reverted to the public sector when the banks that had extended credit to them were brought under state control.

Debt equity swap is another popular mode of finance. Here the debt holder who wants to buy the enterprise exchanges debt worth a fraction of its face value, in the secondary market, for equity.

Privatization is sometimes defended on the ground of widening share ownership. Experience shows that ownership tends to reconcentrate over time, despite attempts to attract and retain small shareholders. The temptation to make quick cash profit by selling off shares is at fault. This happened in Chile, Malaysia, the UK, and many other countries.

PUBLIC SECTOR REFORM IN INDIA

Our national planners assigned to the public sector a key role in the Indian economy. In line with the professed objective of building a socialist pattern of society private enterprise was kept out of some major sectors such as heavy manufacturing, banking, insurance, power, telecommunications, and most forms of transport. In 1993–4 the public sector accounted for close to one-third of GDP, and close to 70 per cent of total employment in the organized sector.

Public sector reform in India has avoided drastic steps like outright privatization on a large scale or closing down of chronically loss-making units, but the process is firmly launched and the government is committed to a progressive dilution of control. The number of industries reserved for the public sector has been brought down from eighteen to six. The list now includes only arms and ammunitions, atomic energy, mineral oils, railway transport, and atomic minerals. The main emphasis has been on improving the functional autonomy of PSEs combined with dilution of the state's equity in them. By 1997–8 proportion of equity varying from 5 per cent to 49 per cent in some fifty enterprises had been sold. A major objective behind these sales was raising revenue for the budget. But here, as in the UK, underpricing of shares was fairly common, enabling private investors to reap huge windfall gains. The Disinvestment Commission, appointed in 1996, recommended the disinvestment of a majority stake along with management control transfer for several PSEs in non-strategic and non-core areas. This trend seems unlikely to be reversed in the near future. The Union Budget of 2001 recommended the closing down of eight PSEs and indicated the rate at which employment will be forced to contract in the state sector over the next few years. This policy has been strongly opposed by critics who rightly point to the high welfare cost of jobloss in an economy like ours where millions are unemployed and which does not have social safety nets. Overstaffing has been a problem no doubt, but it is equally true that its importance has often been exaggerated to hide the failure of managers and bureaucrats. Putting a curb on the rate of growth of employment is one thing but making it negative is quite another.

It is not true that there is no alternative to retrenchment. By giving more autonomy to managers, introducing better incentive systems, and putting more weight on market-oriented performance, it should be possible to turn loss-making units around without retrenching workers. This actually happened when Tata Steel bought OMC Alloys in Orissa in 1991. The new methods of management were so successful in improving the rate of capacity utilization (from 50 per cent to 90 per cent) that productivity rose dramatically along with profits without any change in the workforce. Privatization or any other organizational change in India should be delinked from large scale retrenchment. Also, privatized units should be kept under regulation because capital market control mechanisms that work through take-overs are not very active in India. The managerial labour market is also not well developed.

In the UK most privatized industries showed healthy increases in sales per employee and in returns on capital employed. Employment has declined. For India available data on financial performance of PSEs show that pretax profits as per cent of capital employed has gone up from 3.4 in 1990–1 to 8.1 in 1995–6.

Both the industrial and foreign trade sectors in India before the reforms were under pervasive government control. In industry the licensing system was the major instrument. Under it, permission was needed for new investment as well as for expansion of capacity. In addition, there was the MRTP Act which put more restrictions on large private companies to prevent concentration of economic power. Imports of a wide range of consumption goods were subject to tariffs, quotas, and other restrictions such as exchange controls. All this was part of the overall policy of import-substituting industrialization.

It has to be acknowledged that central planning in India has pro-duced many positive benefits. It has helped the economy to build up impressive technological capability from a narrow base and self-sufficiency has been achieved on several fronts. The record is far better than that of many countries of Africa or Latin America.

But it is also undeniable that the controls have produced serious negative effects. By reducing competition, both internal and foreign, they have led to the creation and perpetuation of monopoly profits or scarcity rents on a significant scale. As a result much real resource has gone into purely rent-seeking activities. A study by Sharif Mohammad and John Whalley ('*Rent Seeking in India: Its Costs and Policy Significance*', Kyklos, 1984) classified rent-seeking activity in India under four major heads—those associated with foreign trade controls, price control in product markets, labour market controls, and capital market subsidies. Their finding is presented in Table 3.2.

A follow-up study on rent seeking after reform and deregulation will be extremely interesting. The vital point to note in this context is that the evil will not automatically disappear if government con-trolled monopolies are converted into private monopolies. The incen-tives for rent seeking will remain just as strong in this case. What is called for, and this is too often forgotten by the champions of free market, is not simple ownership transfer or liberalization, but promo-tion of active competition combined with more effective regulation. It

Table 3.2: Cost of Rent Seeking in India, 1980–1

Category	per cent of GNP
Import licences/Export incentives	3.8
Capital market controls	8.2 – 16.3
Product market controls	16.3 – 20.2
Labour market controls	2.9
Total	29.9 – 43.2

Source: Mohammad and Whalley (1984).

is in recognition of this that the Government of India has set up a body like the Telecommunications Regulatory Authority of India (TRAI) to oversee the decontrolled telecommunications industry. Regulation cannot be perfect. Attempt should be to make it as efficient as possible, not to do away with it altogether. Unregulated monopoly may entail very substantial social costs. The gain in dynamic efficiency and product quality, if any, may well be outweighed by allocative inefficiency and the adverse impact on the distribution of income and wealth.

A CASE STUDY OF LIBERALIZATION OF TELECOMMUNICATIONS IN INDIA

The decision to liberalize basic telecommunications and value added services (cellular phones and pagers) was taken in May 1994.

In the pre-reform days the basic services were provided by the Department of Telecommunications (DoT) and two government run units: Videsh Sanchar Nigam Limited (VSNL) in charge of international telecom and Mahanagar Telephone Nigam Limited (MTNL) which provided local service in the major cities. Extremely high price (by international standards) enabled both VSNL and MTNL to earn substantial profits. At the same time, DoT employed about fifty workers per 1000 links in comparison with five to ten employees per 1000 links by the efficient companies worldwide.

For cellular mobile phone services private entry was allowed on the basis of open tenders after the government had announced the fixed licence fee beforehand and private firms competed in terms of rental charges to consumers. In the first stage only Mumbai, Delhi, Kolkata, and Chennai were included. In the second stage the rest of the country was divided into nineteen circles of three categories A, B, and C. Two highest bidders were to be granted licence in each circle.

The major eligibility conditions were: (a) the bidder must be a registered Indian company; (b) total foreign equity in the company must not exceed 49 per cent; and (c) net worth of the bidder must be at least Rs 1000 million for category A, and Rs 500 million and Rs 300 million for B and C respectively. Afterwards, the Ministry changed some rules to restrict monopoly power and consequently there was rebidding in some circles.

For paging services licences were given for a period of ten years on competitive bidding and by June 1995 private firms were active in twenty-five cities.

For basic telecom services tenders were invited for twenty-one circles into which the country was divided excluding the MTNL cities. The eligibility criteria were almost the same as in the case of cellular phone services. Private firms were allowed to operate local and STD services within the circles. The inter-circle STD and international services were to remain with DoT and VSNL respectively.

After the auctions were held the government made two moves that threw the entire process into confusion and led to rebidding in no less than thirteen circles. It decided to: (a) fix a cap of three circles per bidder (after a single company Himachal Futuristic Communications Limited had won nine out of twenty circles); and (b) reject the highest bid on ten circles on the ground that they were below the reservation price, although no such price was announced beforehand.

The government's moves were designed to ensure that the winners did not enjoy excessive monopoly profits. They were also prompted by observations that seemed to indicate collusion among bidders. The government, however, should have anticipated this at the stage of designing the auction itself. Ex post decision changes lead to wastage of resources and revenue loss. Designing an appropriate auction mechanism keeping in mind the strategic response of bidders is not an easy task. In particular, revisions and retractions should be kept to a minimum. Underhand deals leading to irregularities in the tendering process were, unfortunately, not entirely absent. In several circles companies reacted by moving the Supreme Court. Greater transparency must be ensured in all the stages of the liberalization process to keep a strict check on possible rent-seeking behaviour.

PROPER ROLE OF THE STATE

It should be reiterated that although state intervention, carried to excess and crudely implemented, can seriously hamper the programme of economic development it does not follow that any positive role for the state in the economy is ruled out thereby. Very simply put, market failure is not automatically eliminated by the fact of government failure. So long as it is possible for the free market equilibrium to diverge from the social optimum due to the presence of externalities and exercise of market power by sellers or buyers (in factor markets), corrective measures cannot be done away with.

An even more important role for the government is in the sphere of redistribution of income and wealth. The consequence will be socially disastrous if distribution is entirely left to be determined by market forces. Even mainstream economic theory admits that the market mechanism is the appropriate instrument for promoting economic efficiency but not for improving income distribution. The first fundamental theorem of welfare economics states that under certain conditions competitive equilibrium leads to Pareto efficiency but says nothing about the desirability of the resulting outcome from the distributional point of view. According to the second theorem, which is a sort of converse, any desirable efficient solution can be realized through the market provided that the initial distribution of resource endowments is appropriately adjusted. In either case government intervention is theoretically justified.

The much talked about trade off between equity and efficiency may be a false one (or at least not valid over the entire range), because too much inequality is bound to have an adverse impact on efficiency. A complementary rather than inverse relationship between growth and equality has indeed been observed for East Asian countries. If globalization leads to worsening of the position of the poor and the underprivileged, absolutely and relatively, social stability may be disrupted and growth may cease to be sustainable even if supported by clean technologies that protect the environment and conserve natural resources. Intensification of income inequality may well be the worst kind of pollution and negative externality generated by industrial progress. To counter this, redistributive systems such as progressive taxation of income and wealth, and social security nets will have to be maintained and effectively administered. That governments have often failed to use them effectively is no reason for their abolition.

More open economies have greater exposure to risks emanating from disturbances in world markets. Governments, therefore, have to play an insulation function, providing safety and security in terms of employment as well as purchases from the rest of the economy.

Benefit accrues to both labour and domestic business. The post-war expansion of multilateral trade was accompanied everywhere by strong, stabilizing governments at home. Neoliberalism today is, however, denying any proactive role to the state, which means less regulation and less stabilization. But in a country such as ours, where social safety nets are inadequate and labour is generally much more vulnerable than capital owing to weaker economic position and less mobility, the sheltering function of the government sector can never be done away with.

The naive 'market versus state' debate of the 1980s has now been supplanted by the recognition that both, the market and the state, are indispensable for a successful liberalization programme. The major task now is to find a proper combination of the two imperfect mechanisms. The public sector has to be reoriented so that it gets out of activities where the state has no comparative advantage (such as hotels, tourism, and production of scooters or tractors) and concentrate on building up social capital in the fields of education, infrastructure, public health, and agricultural support services.

Competitive markets are a means to achieve certain ends and like all instruments markets should be evaluated by judging whether they promote our social and economic goals. It has been rightly observed that 'markets, free or otherwise, are not a product of nature. On the contrary, markets are legally constructed instruments, created by human beings hoping to produce a successful system of social ordering...there is no opposition between "markets" and "government intervention". Markets are (a particular form of) government intervention.' (Sunstein 1997).

The quality of governance has become the key variable in explaining the economic performance of nations. In its 1992 'Report on Governance and Development' the World Bank defined governance as 'the manner in which power is exercised in the management of a country's economic and social resources for development'. Political organization and administrative competence of governments have been singled out as the crucial explanatory factor in several studies of comparative development experience. An important study of around one hundred countries over 1960–90 by Robert Barro has highlighted that economic growth is stimulated by better schooling and life expectancy, lower fertility, lower government consumption, and better maintenance of the rule of law. Good institutions are the best capital that a society can have and the state should focus on the difficult task of creating and sustaining them. Overreliance on the state has led to the discovery of the market in the developing world, unregulated capitalism will soon force a rediscovery of the state in a modified form.

APPENDIX

Welfare Comparison of Different Market Structures

Suppose that the market demand function is linear, $P = a - q$. In duopoly $q = q_1 + q_2$, where q_1, q_2 are the outputs of the two firms. Let the cost functions be

$$C_i = cq_i, i = 1, 2.$$

Also assume $a > c$. There is no fixed cost. The profit function for the ith firm is

$$\pi_i = [a - (q_1 + q_2) - c] q_i.$$

The reaction function of firm 1 is obtained from $\partial \pi_1 / \partial q_1 = 0$. This yields

$$a - c - 2q_1 - q_2 = 0 \text{ or } q_1 = (a - c - q_2) / 2.$$

Similarly, the reaction function of firm 2 obtained from

$$\partial \pi_2 / \partial q_2 = 0 \text{ is } q_2 = (a - c - q_1) / 2.$$

The Cournot equilibrium, given by the solution of the two reaction function equations, is

$q_1^* = q_2^* = (a - c)/3$, $P^* = (a + 2c)/3$. The profits are $\pi_1^* = \pi_2^* = (a - c)^2/9$

Consumers' surplus (CS) is the triangular area below the demand curve and above the price line. $CS = 2 (a - c)^2/9$
Social welfare in Cournot duopoly is:

$$W_D = CS + \pi_1^* + \pi_2^* = 4(a - c)^2/9$$

In perfect competition, $P = MC = c$, so that $q = a - c$ and $CS = (a - c)^2/2$. Since $MC = AC$ firms make zero profits. Therefore, $W_C = CS = (a - c)^2/2$.

A monopoly determines this equilibrium by setting $MR = MC$ or $q-2q = c$. The solution is,

$q = (a - c)/2$, $P = (a + c) / 2$. Profit is, $\pi_m = (a - c)^2/4$.

$$W_m = CS + \pi_m = 3(a - c)^2/8$$

Therefore, the welfare ranking is:

$$W_C > W_D > W_M$$

Competition is the best, monopoly the worst, with duopoly in between. It is to be noted that monopoly profit π_m is greater than the combined profit of the two firms in duopoly $(1/4 > 2/9)$. This makes collusion mutually profitable.

n-firm oligopoly

If there are n-firms in an oligopoly the reaction function of the ith firm is of the form $(a - c) - [2q_i + \Sigma q_{-i}] = 0$
where Σq_{-i} is the sum of outputs of all firms except firm i
 If the firms are identical each will produce the same output in equilibrium, that is, $q_i^* = q^*$, $i = 1, 2, ..., n$.
 The above equation yields

$$(a - c) - [2q^* + (n - 1) q^*] = 0 \text{ or } q^* = (a - c)/n + 1.$$

As n becomes larger and larger industry output nq^* tends to $(a - c)$, the competitive output and price tends to c, the marginal cost.

Industry Concentration

Let us consider the general market demand function, $P = f(q)$, $f' < 0$.
 The cost function of the ith firm is $C_i = c_i q_i$, so that MC and AC now differ across firms. Profit maximization by firm i implies

$$(d\pi_i)/(dq_i) = d/dq_i (Pq_i - C_i q_i) = P + q_i (dP/dq).(dq/dq_i) - c_i = 0$$

Under Cournot assumption, $(dq/dq_i) = 1$.
 Using $e = -(P/q)(dq/dP)$ and market share of firm i, $s_i = (q_i / q)$, the above equation can be rewritten as,

$$P\{1 - (s_i / e)\} = c_i \text{ or } (P - c_i) / P = (s_i / e)$$

Multiplying both sides by s_i, summing for all firms and using $H = \Sigma s_i^2$ we get

$$(P\Sigma s_i - \Sigma s_i c_i)/P = H/e \text{ or } (P - \bar{c})/P = H/e$$

where $\bar{c}$ is the share weighted mean MC for the industry.

Averch–Johnson Effect

Let the production function be $q = f(L, K)$ and P, w, r the fixed prices of the product and the two inputs, labour and capital. Operating profit relative to the capital base is restricted to a maximum rate of return of s. Viability needs $s > r$. The seller's problem is to choose levels of L and K to maximise profit

$$P f(L, K) - wL - rK \text{ subject to } (P f(L, K) - wL) / K \leq s.$$

Setting $P = 1$, the Lagrangean is

$$L = f(L, K) - wL - rK + m (sK - f(L, K) + wL)$$

Assuming the constraint to hold with equality, the first order conditions are

$$(f_L - w)(1 - m) = 0$$

$$f_K - r + ms - mf_K = 0$$

From the second equation,

$$m = (r - f_K) / (s - f_K) < 1, \text{ by } s > r.$$

We also have

$$\frac{f_K}{f_L} = \frac{r - ms}{(1 - m)w} < \frac{r}{w}$$

Therefore, the regulated firm faces a distorted factor price ratio that induces it to push the use of K beyond the level that minimises cost at market prices w and r.

FOUR

Multinational Corporations and Direct Foreign Investment

This chapter takes a close look at MNCs and DFI, concepts that have become household words under the sway of liberalization and globalization. Reasons behind the spectacular rise of these giants and the spurt in foreign investment by them are analysed. The benefits they can confer through technology transfer and quality upgradation and as a source of external funds are set out, as is their potential negative impact on the host economy. The negative factors operate through transfer pricing and adverse competition effects. The current liberalized DFI policy of our government is discussed.

DEFINITION AND IMPORTANCE

An MNC is an enterprise that spreads its operations over many nations by owning and controlling production facilities outside its home country. It is essential that productive capacity is not located in a single country. In other words, a company that produces in one place and exports to other countries does not qualify as an MNC, no matter how large is the number of export markets served or how big is the total value of the exports.

Overseas ownership may be achieved either by taking over local enterprises (mergers and acquisitions/takeovers) or by investing directly in new capacity creation (greenfield site investment). All MNCs combine in various degrees vertical integration (different stages of the same production activity taking place in different countries) and horizontal integration (performing the same operation in different countries).

MNCs differ from their domestic counterparts in one important respect, namely, their exposure to international risks. This includes exchange rate risk (an American multinational may find that the earnings of its subsidiary in London have shrunk suddenly in dollars as a result of a fall in the value of the pound vis-à-vis the dollar) and the threat of expropriation (nationalization) of foreign assets following a change of political regime in the host country. Another problem is that of double taxation of profit—once in the country where it is originally earned and again in the home country when it is repatriated.

About one-fifth of the total world GNP is currently produced by the MNCs. For some individual countries their share in GNP exceeds one-third. Approximately one-fourth of the global trade consists of trade between subsidiaries or branches within MNCs. Indeed they are rapidly replacing countries as the largest economic units in the global market. The ten largest non-financial MNCs ranked by assets in 1997 are listed in Table 4.1.

Table 4.1: The Top Ten Non-financial MNCs, 1997

Name	Home	Industry	Asset	Sales	World
			(US$ billion)		employment
General Electric	USA	Electronics	304	908	276,000
Ford Motor	USA	Motor vehicles	275.4	153.6	364,000
General Motors	USA	Motor vehicles	228.9	178.2	608,000
Royal Dutch/ Shell	UK/Holland	Oil	115	128	105,000
Toyota	Japan	Motor vehicles	105	88.5	160,000
Exxon	USA	Oil	96.1	120.3	80,000
IBM	USA	Computer	81.5	78.5	269,500
Daimler–Benz	Germany	Motor vehicles	76.2	69	300,000
Volkswagen group	Germany	Motor vehicles	57	65	280,000
Nestle	Switzerland	Food & beverage	37.7	48.3	226,000

Source: UNCTAD, World Investment Reports (1997, 1999).

The nationality of the world's top 100 multinationals has hardly changed over the decades. No less than 89 per cent are headquartered in the triad of the EU, the USA, and Japan. In 1997 about two-thirds of the companies were from just four industries—motor vehicles, electronics and electrical equipment, petroleum, and pharmaceuticals.

Only two companies from the developing world, Petroleos de Venezuela (Venezuela) and Daewoo Corporation (South Korea) figure in the list of the globally top hundred MNCs. The set of top fifty developing country MNCs is dominated by firms from a small group of countries—Hong Kong (China), South Korea, Venezuela, Mexico, and Brazil, which account for almost 80 per cent of the foreign assets of the set.

Since 1990 United Nation's Conference on Trade and Development (UNCTAD) has been computing an index of transnationality for MNCs to measure the importance of foreign assets, sales, and employment in their overall activities. The average index of the top hundred corporations has been steadily increasing over the past decade. For the fifty largest companies from the LDCs the upward trend in average transnationality index suffered a serious setback in 1997 in the wake of the financial crisis.

Table 4.2a: Top Ten Non-financial MNCs Ranked by Transnationality Index and Foreign Assets, 1997

Name	Foreign assets (US$ billion)	TI
General Electric	97.4	84
Ford Motor Company	72.5	80
Royal Dutch/Shell	70.0	44
General Motors	60.0	91
Exxon Corporation	54.6	29
Toyota	41.8	75
IBM	39.9	54
Volkswagen Group	36.0	50
Nestle	31.6	4
Daimler–Benz	30.9	71

Note: TI = Transnationality Index

Source: UNCTAD, *World Investment Reports* (1997, 1999).

Table 4.2b: Top Ten Developing Country MNCs Ranked by
Transnationality Index and Foreign Assets, 1997

Name	Country	Foreign assets (US$ million)	TI
Petroleos de Venezuela	Venezuela	9007	12
Daewoo Corporation	South Korea	7500	10
Jardine Matheson Ltd.	Hongkong, China	6652	4
First Pacific Co. Ltd.	Hongkong, China	6295	5
Cemex	Mexico	5627	9
Hutchison Whampoa Ltd.	Hongkong, China	4978	17
China State Construction Co.	China	3730	29
China National Chemicals Import & Export Co.	China	3460	14
LG Electronics	South Korea	3159	23
YPF Sociedad Anonima	Argentina	3061	35

Note: TI = Transnationality Index
Source: UNCTAD, *World Investment Reports* (1997, 1999).

DIRECT FOREIGN INVESTMENT

DFI is long term international capital movement of a particular type.
(Capital movement does not imply physical movement of machines
and equipment. It refers to movement of investible funds or finance.)
If the lender, that is, purchaser of the productive asset, has operating
control over the asset's use then investment is direct, otherwise it is
portfolio. One can acquire control by buying enough shares of common stock in a company. If, instead, the lender chooses to buy bonds
issued by the firm he receives interest income but acquires no share
in ownership and cannot participate in decision-making irrespective
of the value of the bonds purchased. When the term DFI is used in
connection with MNCs it implies buying or building and operating
subsidiaries and wholly or partially owned affiliates in foreign
countries.

DFI has grown spectacularly since 1945. Although the bulk of it
has taken place within the developed world, the pattern is beginning
to change with the rapid economic growth in the countries of South
and East Asia.

Over the next twenty-five years the current ranking of the world's
top fifteen economies is projected to undergo substantial change. In

Table 4.3: Annual Average DFI Flow to LDCs by Region

(US$ million)

	1990–2	1993	1994	1995
All Developing Countries	35,532	79,576	80,120	90,346
Asia	16,024	46,427	44,279	55,749
East Asia–Pacific	15,509	44,871	43,037	53,703
South Asia	515	1376	1242	2046
Latin America and the Caribbean	11,638	18,104	20,811	17,799
Middle East and North Africa	2221	3189	3681	2129

Source: Various World Bank reports.

1992 the economies ranked by GNP (an index of market size) were: the USA, Japan, China, Germany, France, India, Italy, the UK, Russia, Brazil, Mexico, Indonesia, Canada, Spain, and South Korea. In 2020—assuming the countries grow at the rates projected by the World Bank—this set is likely to change to: China, the USA, Japan, India, Indonesia, Germany, South Korea, Thailand, France, Taiwan, Brazil, Italy, Russia, the UK, and Mexico. It follows that MNCs will be increasingly drawn to countries such as China, India, Indonesia, South Korea, and Thailand. Vastly improved communications technology that has led to a sharp reduction in the costs of doing business across national boundaries will be a big factor assisting such a move.

According to World Bank figures net DFI flow to LDCs increased from US$ 10.4 billion (1986) to US$ 35 billion (1991) and US$ 80 billion (1994). The share of the LDCs in total DFI jumped from 12 per cent in 1990 to 37 per cent in 1997. It has subsequently declined to 28 per cent. China is by far the largest recipient of this flow. Figures for China contain an upward bias due to substantial recycling of domestic funds through Hong Kong and Macao in order to take advantage of concessions given to foreign investors.

Another factor that will significantly stimulate the growth of DFI is the rapidly rising importance of services in international trade. This is because provision of most services like banking, insurance, transportation, and consultancy requires presence in the customer's vicinity. In activities such as accounting, advertising, and insurance sales by US affiliates abroad already far outweigh direct exports by US corporations. Over the decade of the 1990s some 50 per cent of the global stock of DFI was in service activities. To quote from a report of UNCTAD (1994):

In the FDI area liberalization is the most important policy trend of the 1990s, as part of broadbased efforts to attract foreign investors. This trend is embedded in a broader liberalization movement—covering international trade in goods, external financial transactions, transfer of technology, and, more recently, services and some aspects of labour movement—that seeks to enhance economic efficiency through the elimination of market distortions caused by restrictions or discriminatory governmental measures. These policies are interrelated and mutually supportive.

The trend towards the liberalization of regulatory regimes for DFI continues apace across the globe. Out of approximately one hundred and fifty regulatory changes relating to DFI made during 1998 by sixty countries, 94 per cent were aimed at creating more favourable environment for MNCs. The number of bilateral investment agreements among countries are also steadily on the rise. Close to 40 per cent of the agreements signed in 1998 was between developing countries.

DFI outflow from the developing countries has also been on the rise over the past twenty years. This is a reflection of the growing competitiveness of MNCs from the LDCs which enables them to invest abroad. Most of this outflow goes to countries in East and South East Asia, especially to the members of the Association of South East Asian Nations (ASEAN). The 'first wave' of DFI outflow from the developing world that took place in the 1960s and the 1970s originated in Argentina, Brazil, Chile, Mexico, and Venezuela. It was mainly of the market-seeking type attempting to overcome trade barriers in the host countries. The Latin American firms were swamped in the 1980s by the 'second wave' that was led by Asian companies. They have re-emerged as leaders in the 'third wave' of the 1990s driven by programmes of structural adjustment and reform including trade liberalization, privatization, and deregulation. At present, Cemex (Mexico) is the world's second largest producer of cement with plants in the USA, Europe, and Asia and Techint (Argentina) accounts for 30 per cent of global market for seamless pipes for the petroleum industry and operates a network in Argentina, Mexico, and Italy.

UNCTAD has also devised an index of transnationality for nations to measure the extent to which any host country is involved in international production. It is based on the following four ratios: a) DFI inflow as a percentage of gross fixed capital formation for the past three years; b) DFI stock as a percentage of GDP; c) value added of foreign affiliates as a percentage of GDP; and d) share of foreign affiliates in total employment. A recent report reveals that among the DCs New Zealand has the highest transnationality index and Japan the lowest. Among the LDCs Trinidad and Tobago tops the list while India is close to the bottom. China's position is much higher.

WHY GO GLOBAL?

MNCs in extractive industries like oil, aluminium, or copper obviously have to set up base where the minerals are located. In most other cases the high level of transfer costs (costs of moving goods across national boundaries consisting of shipping cost, import duties and other trade taxes, and various administrative expenses) make it more profitable to shift production overseas. Threat of trade related retaliatory measures prompted Japanese automakers to set up plants in the USA and the UK. American MNCs undertook DFI in several European countries to gain a firm foothold before the EU could succeed in building an impregnable 'Fortress Europe'. But all these factors do not explain why foreign firms are better able to exploit

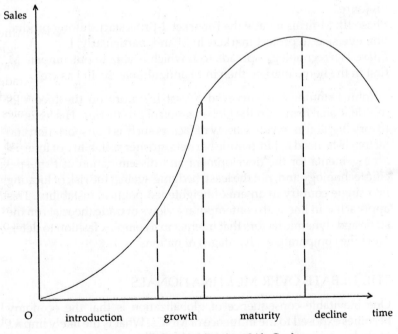

Figure 4.1: Typical Product Life Cycle

local advantages than domestic ones. Why were the oil fields of the Middle East developed by the American, British, and Dutch companies? Here the technological and managerial advantages of MNCs became decisive. These advantages, in turn, are due to early start, successful research and development, learning by doing, and exploitation of economies of scale. Owing to their reputation and market power it is also far easier for them to raise finance for market exploration and further investment.

Firms often decide to go global in order to extend the life cycle of their products. Figure 4.1 shows a typical product life cycle.

A product may be at different stages of its life cycle in different geographic localities and this makes multinationalization of production and sales profitable. Consider three countries, the innovator (I), the medium cost land (M), and the low cost LDC (L).

Phase I: Production is concentrated in I which exports to other countries.

Phase II: As production technique becomes standardized and the I market matures, production starts in M. Local producers first displace imports from I and then start exporting to L. I-firms are under pressure.

Phase III: M-firms invade the I-market. I-firms start shifting production overseas to protect markets in M and, particularly, L.

Phase IV: Technology spreads to L which is able to outcompete M, first in the home market, then in M and, ultimately, in I as well.

John Dunning has surveyed a vast literature on the theory of multinational firms and the globalization of production. His 'eclectic' theory highlights a wide variety of factors such as transportation and factor costs, need to jump trade barriers, greater suitability of internal arrangements for the development and dissemination of firm-specific technology and, not the least, hedging against the risk of locating in a single country in an era of heightened political instability. This approach is in line with contemporary views of trade theorists on the static and dynamic factors that interact in a complex fashion to determine the comparative advantages of nations.

THE DEBATE OVER MULTINATIONALS

One inevitable consequence of globalization is that the economy becomes exposed to the influence of MNCs. What is the likely impact of such exposure on a country's welfare? This question continues to be intensely and hotly debated, particularly in the LDCs currently going through extensive economic reform.

Advocates of liberalization are also by and large supporters of MNCs. They argue that by bringing in new technologies, marketing skills, and organizational techniques such investment will help in restructuring by imparting much needed dynamism to the stagnant industrial sector. Diffusion of the new technology and management methods to the domestic firms is bound to occur without any significant lag. It is pointed out that in the UK car industry (including its suppliers) there was a general improvement in performance after Japanese MNCs like Nissan had introduced and insisted on stricter quality control standards. Similar effects were observed in many European and some Latin American countries. This was followed by growth of employment and real wages in the sectors where DFI has taken place.

The World Bank also never tires of repeating the virtues of DFI-led export oriented growth. Add to this the general disillusionment with inward oriented import-substituting industrial policy and it is easy to see why national as well as regional governments the world over are now vying with one another to woo foreign investors. Competition is intense in terms of concessions (tax credits, lower regulatory control, etc.) offered. In India the state governments of Karnataka and Andhra Pradesh have taken the most initiative in this respect.

The critics of MNCs vehemently oppose such practice, saying that they give an unfair competitive edge to foreign companies that already enjoy several advantages over smaller domestic firms. There is every possibility that domestic firms will be driven out of business and the already bleak employment scene will be further depressed. However, if the MNCs establish a strong link with domestic suppliers of intermediate inputs then the induced growth in this sector may offset the decline in employment in firms that compete directly with the more powerful MNCs. In a recent survey of multinationals *The Economist* magazine remarked:

Too many governments see foreign investment as a shortcut to prosperity, bringing in skill, capital and technology to push their countries rapidly from the 1950s to the 1990s. Those governments that rely too heavily on multinationals are likely to look for a foreign scapegoat when inflation heads for triple figures, unemployment fails to drop and demonstrators surround the ministry.

Strong linkage with domestic suppliers can serve as an effective conduit for technology transfer. The MNCs, however, may not take any initiative to establish and foster such linkage, particularly if DFI is of the tariff-jumping type. This is the situation where an MNC sets up a plant in a foreign country because direct export to that country has to face stiff tariff barriers. Then its tendency will be to import part finished products from its home base (on which duty is lower) and use cheap local labour to assemble the final product. In the production plants set up by Volkswagen in Brazil in the 1970s workers assembled 'complete knockdown kits' into cars that were sold tariff-free in Brazil. To prevent such screwdriver operation most countries now impose local content requirements under which MNCs are obliged to use a minimum amount (as percentage of value) of goods and services of local origin as intermediate inputs.

Critics also heavily discount the alleged technology transfer benefit of MNCs. Since technical superiority is one of the most powerful factors that made overseas expansion so profitable in the first place, a rational MNC can be expected to ensure that such advantage is not dissipated too soon. This is the chief reason why setting up a subsidiary is preferred to licensing the patented technology to a domestic firm.

MNCs can contribute significantly to growth in exports through two channels. First, they supply the technology and skills needed to supplement local resources and second, they provide access to international markets. The intra-MNC market itself is immense, to which access is available only to affiliates. Since the major distribution channels worldwide are controlled by these companies, without their active participation it may be extremely difficult to market even good quality, cost competitive products. They can also influence the granting of trade opportunities in their home countries or sometimes even in third markets. This explains why many LDCs today are trying to enlist the help of the MNCs in creating the base from which they hope to launch a successful career in exports.

Perhaps the most serious charge against MNCs is that they can (and often do) act in ways that impair the autonomy of the host country's government. It is difficult to impose regulatory control over these companies because they can pack up and relocate elsewhere, which may be costly for the host country. Often their activities act as a constraint on the government's pursuit of national policy objectives. For example, the spread of multinational banking has seriously eroded the effectiveness of monetary and fiscal policies by improving dramatically the international mobility of capital. More serious and irksome is the fact that MNCs often get involved in political battles.

After the Iranian militants had seized the American embassy in Tehe-ran in 1979 the US government instructed American banks all over the world to freeze the accounts of Iranian depositors. The British government objected, saying that Washington has to seek its permission before issuing orders to US banks operating in London. This action was also strongly resented by the international banking community. According to one poll, two-thirds of bankers, including Americans, disapproved. Sometimes MNCs themselves take the initiative in instigating political action. In the early 1970s when the Chilean subsidiaries of International Telephone and Telegraph Company were finding the policies of President Allende rather unpalatable, the company found ways of inducing the US government to adopt strong anti-Allende measures.

MNCs are often guilty of fixing intra-company transactions to minimize their global tax bill or to get around restrictions on profit remittance. Transfer pricing is the means of doing it. Transfer prices are those that the various divisions of an MNC charge each other. They are entirely internal to the company. (The problem of transfer pricing is not restricted to affiliates. It may equally arise in joint ventures.) Consider a company that operates in two countries. Division A (situated in country A) produces an intermediate product with market value of Rs 50. Cost of production is Rs 40, so that profit of this division is Rs 10. Division B (situated in country B) 'purchases' the intermediate product from Division A, adds value to it and sells the final product for Rs 120. Let its cost of operation be Rs 40. The profit of Division B is Rs 30 (= 120 – 50 – 40). In country A the corporate tax rate is 10 per cent while in B it is 50 per cent. If the company declares its true profits its total tax liability will be Rs 16 (Re 1 in A and Rs 15 in B).

Consider a situation where the company assigns a transfer price of Rs 60 (higher than the true value of Rs 50) to its product manufactured in the low tax country A. Division A now shows a profit of Rs 20 and faces tax liability of Rs 2. Division B's 'profit' goes down from Rs 30 to Rs 20 (=120 – 60 – 40), tax falls from Rs 15 to Rs 10. Total tax liability on the global operation is now only Rs 12, instead of Rs 16. Thus merely by shifting its profit from the high tax country to the low tax one through transfer pricing, the company has succeeded in pushing up its global after-tax profits. Understandably, the government of country B will not feel too happy about it. Detection of inflated transfer prices is possible when there is an active market for the intermediate product in the country of final sales, so that the tax authorities can refer to the going market price. But such markets often do not exist.

A Monopolies and Mergers Commission Report revealed that in the UK in 1973 a Swiss pharmaceutical company set prices for two intermediate products at £370 and £922 per kilogram at a time when the current market prices for the same two products were £9 and £20 per kilogram respectively. During the 1980s California, Montana, and some other high-tax states in the USA refused to accept the MNCs' declaration of profits earned and imposed 'unitary taxation' which assumed that the share of a company's profit earned in the state equals the state's share of the firm's global sales or payroll. Under pressure from the MNCs and the US federal government the system had to be finally abandoned.

It is, however, not the case that national governments have completely given up attempts to check transfer pricing. In 1994 tax authorities in the USA made income adjustments of US$ 2 billion and US$ 1.5 billion for 236 non-US controlled and 156 US controlled MNCs respectively. In Japan, in 1997, about one hundred adjustments to reported income of multinationals were made, the total coming to US$ 350 million. Similar action has been taken in the EU too. With the liberalization of remittances and reduction in corporate tax rates by numerous LDCs the incidence of transfer pricing may have declined in recent years. Double taxation treaties between home and host countries have also contributed.

The impact of DFI on the economy of the host country depends crucially on how it is financed. Suppose an American firm establishes its subsidiary in India with funds raised in the USA. This will constitute a capital inflow into India. But if the fund is raised locally by selling bonds in the Indian money market no capital movement takes place. The DFI simply crowds out local investment. To prevent this from happening, Chile, even after substantial liberalization of policy towards DFI, has retained the right to limit the access of foreign companies to the domestic banking system. Although it has never been invoked, the very presence of the provision is a reminder of the possibility of crowding out. (Apart from finance, crowding out may operate through the decision of skilled personnel to join the MNCs because of their reputation or more attractive emoluments.)

There is also a difference between takeover and greenfield site investment. In the case of takeover total capital stock does not change immediately, only ownership changes. The capital stock will eventually change as a result of new investment policy. Employment will be stimulated if the MNC succeeds in turning around a non-performing enterprise after taking it over.

MULTINATIONALS AND COMPETITION EFFECTS

The entry and operations of an MNC into the market of a host country is likely to impact significantly on its structure, conduct, and performance. First, these markets become more contestable, if we take 'contestability' to mean ease of entry and openness to competition rather than low sunk costs as in contestability theory. The immediate reaction of local firms to inward DFI is expected to be an attempt to motivate the management and the employees to reduce organizational slack and improve X-efficiency. To the extent that they succeed it is an efficiency gain for the whole society. It is also not uncommon for the local firms to adopt the superior production techniques of the foreign entrant. However, it is not easy to generalize about the impact on local producers and their reactions, as revealed by the following examples:

- In Brazil's textile industry introduction of synthetic fibres by an MNC led to stagnation of demand for cotton textiles and a number of local firms had to close down. Some others survived by entering into joint ventures with foreign firms to obtain access to modern technology.

- A favourable patent protection regime, strict import controls, and licensing restrictions since the 1970s had enabled the Indian pharmaceutical industry to build up considerable technological capabilities. Now, faced with the threat of foreign entry under a liberalized trade and investment regime, they are gearing up to meet the challenge by increasing investment to improve their own R&D and marketing capabilities.

- The experience of the Brazilian telecommunication equipment industry shows that domestic firms may find it very difficult to compete with foreign affiliates even when technical capability is well developed. Liberalization of DFI and entry of affiliates forced a number of local sellers to reduce their R&D activities and enter into alliances and joint ventures, often on very unfavourable terms. This was because they were finding it impossible to compete with the foreign affiliates who had adopted a policy of rapid introduction of new products. They were successful because they had the products developed by their parent firms to draw upon. Lacking comparable technical and financial backstopping from parent companies, Brazilian firms, particularly the smaller ones, were left with cooperation with

---

BOX 4.1: DFI and Competition in the Indian Soft Drink and Domestic Appliances Market

Pepsi entered the market in 1990 with a 44 per cent share in joint venture and subsequently increased it substantially by purchasing the share held by its partner, Voltas Ltd. The remaining 8 per cent was held by the Indian firm, Punjab Agro Industries. In 1993 Coca Cola re-entered the scene after an absence of sixteen years. This was also a joint venture with Parle, which agreed to make available to Coke all of its sixty franchises for production, bottling, and distribution. The decision was to invest US$ 20 million to upgrade Parle's bottling plants. Parle's own cola, Thums Up, was not withdrawn from the market because of its high popularity. Today the two MNCs dominate the lucrative Indian soft drink market (Parle has been taken over by Coca Cola) and spend huge amounts on advertising campaigns. Local competition has been virtually wiped out.

In white goods (washing machines, airconditioners, and refrigerators) the first prominent foreign entrant was Whirlpool Corporation (USA) in 1991. Once again the mode was joint venture with a local firm. By the mid-1990s its market share had already reached a level of 15–20 per cent. The local firm Videocon is finding it increasingly difficult to compete with MNCs such as Whirlpool, Samsung, LG, and Electrolux.

In 1994 Whirlpool acquired a majority stake of 51 per cent in Kelvinator of India, the country's second largest manufacturer of refrigerators at that time. It chose to acquire the use of the Kelvinator brand name until the end of 1996. Then it began to introduce its own brands, starting with a 310 litre model. Its market share has settled around 25 per cent. Godrej–GE, a joint venture between indigenous Godrej and General Electric of the USA, remains the market leader with a share of 40 per cent. Samsung, LG, and Electrolux also are making their presence felt more and more in this expanding market. Competition among the oligopolists has provided the Indian consumer with a wider choice as regards refrigerators.

Source: Economic Times, Business India, World Investment Reports, various issues.

---

the MNCs as the only option for survival. The impact was negative on local innovative capacity.

Numerous studies for individual, developing as well as developed, economies indicate positive correlation between MNC activity and concentration of sellers in the industries of the host countries. The implication for social welfare is negative, because greater concentration usually implies greater market power in the sense of the ability to set prices above marginal costs. This calls for a close watch on the activities of incoming MNCs, something which most LDC governments are not very keen to do right now. What is worse, some governments are indeed so anxious to attract DFI that in exchange for investment they actually agree to offer MNCs various kinds of arrangements that grant enhanced market power with legal protection against competition from domestic firms or other rival MNCs. This will entirely negate the positive contestability effect mentioned earlier.

IMPACT OF CAPITAL INFLOW

The outcome of DFI in most cases depends critically on the bargaining power and skill of the host vis-à-vis international investors. But here, unfortunately, bargaining power is very asymmetrically distributed with most of the strategic and informational advantage lying with the giant multinationals. The options are more limited for the countries, particularly the less developed ones. They may have alternative foreign investors, but they are often unaware of them.

Insofar as the BoP is concerned, DFI (capital inflow) allows the country to run a current account deficit in the short run. Investment may exceed national savings without loss of international reserves. Indeed, as a source of external finance to supplement domestic savings DFI has one major advantage. Being based on a longer term view of the market, it is much less prone to abrupt reversals than bank lending and portfolio investment. The risk of herd behaviour is significantly lower. (Direct investment flows to East Asia remained remarkably stable during the crisis of 1997–8 while portfolio funds and bank debt dried up completely. The situation was similar for Mexico in 1994.) Also, profit repatriation will be low if the project is not successful or if the general performance of the economy is really bad. This constitutes an important advantage over bank lending for which interest must be paid or the principal repaid regardless of the performance of the particular project or the general economy. This factor goes a long way toward explaining the steep jump in the popularity of DFI as a source of external finance in the years following the international debt crisis (see Glossary for more on the debt crisis).

But the ultimate effect on the balance may well be negative if the value of interest, profits, managerial fees, royalty payments, and dividends repatriated (all outflows on current account) exceeds the value of investment. Indeed it can be argued that this condition must hold for any DFI that is based on rational profit calculations. The present value of net profits must be greater than the value of investment. So the ultimate impact on BoPs is bound to be adverse.

It should, however, be pointed out that the economic value of an investment ought not to be assessed by looking only, or even mainly, at its direct impact on the country's BoP. Management of the BoP belongs properly to the realm of macroeconomic policy. Productive DFI will show up in higher growth and under a well-managed foreign trade and exchange rate regime the payments balance will adjust in an appropriate manner.

Even within standard trade theory where the BoP is always in balance and the mode of financing is not an issue, it is possible to show that inflow of foreign capital in a tariff-distorted situation may have an adverse impact on a nation's welfare. Suppose that the country is 'small', so that international prices (its terms of trade) are not affected by its trade. There is a tariff on the importable commodity which is capital intensive. This is a distortion because the optimum trade policy for such a country is free trade or zero tariff. Due to the tariff the production of the importable good is pushed beyond its optimal (free trade) level. If foreign capital comes into this sector the result may be immiserization (decline in welfare). In Figure 4.2 the initial equilibrium is at E with an import tariff in place. The tariff inclusive domestic relative price of the importable good P_t is higher than the world price P_w. Production of the importable under tariff is Y_1, which exceeds its free trade level Y_0. After DFI the production possibility frontier shifts out, but the expansion is biased in favour of Y because the exportable industry X (labour intensive) is relatively less affected by the inflow of capital. The new equilibrium is at E', with a higher output Y_2 of Y but a lower level of welfare. This is not inevitable, but the possibility cannot be ruled out.

The clue to this paradoxical outcome is that DFI is aggravating a distortion that already exists. Output of the protected sector is pushed further away from its best value Y_0. The trade volume at the same time shrinks so much that the final consumption of both goods is smaller than before. A part of the higher GDP now does not accrue to domestic consumers as it is repatriated as profits. (This is not shown in the figure.)

The distinction between GDP (the value of final goods and services

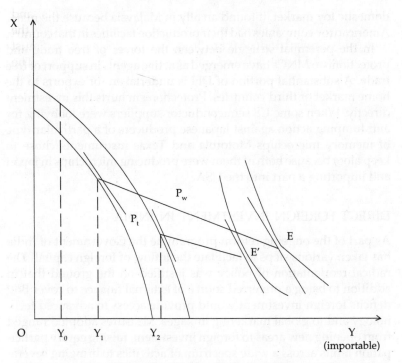

Figure 4.2: Welfare Reducing DFI

produced within the geographic boundary of a nation) and GNP (the income accruing to the citizens of a nation) is important when DFI is in operation. Payments to foreign-owned factors of production are to be subtracted from GDP to arrive at GNP which is the true index of national welfare. Heavy subsidization of DFI over the past two decades has led to impressive GDP growth for Ireland, but the impact on GNP and national welfare has been much less spectacular.

Trade policies can have interesting consequences when MNCs, with their network of production criss-crossing the globe, are involved. A tariff may lose protective power if it induces foreign firms to set up plants in the home country and they sell the product in competition with local firms. When France and Italy decided to set quantitative restrictions on import of Japanese cars the USA was offended because those cars were built in plants in the USA. (Of course, Toyota and Nissan had invested in those plants in the first place to overcome high trade barriers put up by the USA.) On another occasion when the USA was putting pressure on Japan to open up its domestic toy market, it found an ally in Malaysia because the major American toy companies had their production facilities in that country.

In the perennial struggle between the forces of free trade and protectionism MNCs have emerged as active agents in support of free trade. A substantial portion of DFI is undertaken for exports to the home market or third countries. Protectionism hurts this investment directly. When some US semiconductor suppliers were lobbying for antidumping action against Japanese producers of a particular type of memory microchips Motorola and Texas instruments chose to keep aloof because both of them were producing microchips in Japan and importing a part into the USA.

DIRECT FOREIGN INVESTMENT IN INDIA

As part of the ongoing reform programme the Government of India has taken various steps to facilitate the inflow of foreign capital. The radical reorientation of policy was justified on the ground that in addition to being a preferred source of external finance to cover BoP deficits foreign investment would provide access to advanced technology and to global marketing linkages. Measures adopted ranged from opening new areas to foreign investment, raising equity participation limits across a wide spectrum of activities to bringing several sectors under the automatic approval route of the RBI. The target was to attract an average annual inflow of US$ 10 billion. The state of current policy in some important sectors is briefly outlined

Pharmaceuticals

100 per cent foreign investment is permitted under the automatic route for the manufacture of bulk drugs and formulations, except drugs under the licensed category and bulk drugs produced by use of recombinant DNA technology.

Telecom

Foreign equity up to 74 per cent is permitted in internet services providers, radio paging services, and end-to-end bandwidth services. For basic and cellular segments 49 per cent remains the cap on foreign equity.

Banking

Foreign investment up to 49 per cent is allowed on a case-by-case basis subject to approval by the Department of Banking Operations at the RBI. Earlier limits were 20 per cent for DFI and 40 per cent for NRIs.

Defence

Up to 26 per cent foreign equity is permitted in defence production, subject to norms laid down by the Ministry of Defence.

Hotels and Tourism

Participation limit has been raised from 51 per cent to 100 per cent under the automatic route. Earlier condition of disinvestments of 26 per cent stake in favour of Indian partner and/or public over a period of five years is no longer applicable.

Airport Projects

The limit is 74 per cent under the automatic route. The Foreign Investment Promotion Board is empowered to raise it to 100 per cent on a case by case basis.

Development of Townships

100 per cent foreign investment is possible subject to land usage norms laid down by the Urban Development Ministry.

Mass Rapid Transport Systems (MRTS)

Foreign investment up to 100 per cent is permitted under the automatic route. This includes necessary commercial development needs of the MRTS projects.

Table 4.4: DFI Inflow as Percentage of GDP

	1985	1990	1995	1998
Brazil	3.15	1.05	3.10	19.27
China	1.44	2.83	12.54	11.92
India	0.19	0.20	2.30	2.60
Indonesia	1.36	3.10	6.74	2.71
Malaysia	8.07	16.25	10.87	25.85
Mexico	1.26	4.33	13.23	10.68
Pakistan	2.29	3.22	6.53	4.61
Philippines	0.25	4.95	8.88	12.81
South Korea	0.84	0.83	0.98	8.09
Thailand	1.49	6.92	2.96	24.69

Source: Indicators Database, World Bank, Washington, DC.

Table 4.4 shows the situation in selected countries in respect of foreign capital inflow.

The absolute figure for India was US$ 3 billion in 1997–8. Although still low compared to the values for some other countries, it represents a dramatic rise from earlier levels (US$ 600 million in 1993) and the trend is upward. But a big gap persists between approval and actual inflows. Another disturbing feature is that while a very high proportion of approvals is for investment in the core sectors like infrastructure, most of DFI is coming to the consumer goods sector.

For a labour-surplus host country like India where unemployment is a serious problem, DFI will have the most favourable impact under the following conditions:

1. Finance is not raised locally, so that there is no crowding out of domestic investment.
2. The technology used by the subsidiaries is labour intensive or not too capital intensive.
3. There is strong linkage with domestic suppliers ensuring quick learning and technology diffusion.
4. The output is not sold in the domestic market, so that local producers are not adversely affected. This is the logic behind allowing DFI only or mostly in EPZs insulated from the rest of the economy.

The Uruguay Round of GATT negotiation (completed in 1993) for the first time addressed issues relating to trade in services and DFI. The agreement on 'trade related investment measures' (TRIMS) is expected to spur the growth of DFI by limiting the power of governments to impose controls on MNCs. This important matter is taken up again in Chapter 7.

The need for eternal vigilance to ensure that foreign capital does not turn into a disruptive force is dramatically illustrated by the Enron fiasco of recent years.

The US multinational Enron Corporation entered into an agreement with the Maharashtra government to build and operate a power plant, Dabhol Power Corporation, costing around US$ 3 billion. The proposal was approved by both the state and central governments. Investors were guaranteed a minimum return of 16 per cent and the price at which power was to be sold to the Maharashtra State Electricity Board was also fixed. Under fast-track procedure for negotiations with foreign investors in infrastructure, the contract was signed without any competitive bidding. The fixed price and the guaranteed rate

BOX 4.2: DFI and the Indian Software Industry

Citibank was the first foreign company to establish, in 1985, a wholly owned, offshore software company in the Santa Cruz Electronics EPZ in Mumbai. The enterprise proved highly profitable owing to the supply of low-cost skilled labour fluent in English and a time difference between Asia and North America that allowed for almost twenty-four hour workdays.

To start with, most of the work took the form of contracts in which exact specifications were given that left little scope for discretion or creativity to the programmers. There was, therefore, not much scope for skill upgradation.

Texas Instruments set up its export oriented, wholly owned subsidiary in 1986 and Hewlett Packard did the same in Bangalore in 1989. The government came forward to provide adequate infrastructure in the form of telecommunications facilities and high speed satellite links. In 1990–1 quantitative restrictions on imports of intermediate inputs and capital goods for software exports were abolished.

Successful investment by Texas Instruments and Hewlett Packard helped the industry to take off at a critical stage. Since then many domestic firms have appeared on the scene enjoying good reputation for reliable, high quality work at very low costs (by international standards). It is not unusual for them to win contracts for whole projects, rather than specific components, at fairly high points on the value added chain.

Export by the Indian software industry is following a steady upward trend. The five largest companies are domestically owned. Foreign affiliates have been overtaken in terms of export competitiveness within a relatively short period.

of return also came under heavy fire as being excessively generous. Accusations of cost padding and crony capitalism rapidly gathered force. The newly elected state government decided to cancel the project, much to the annoyance of Enron and other foreign investors. Competitive bidding was made compulsory for future contracts. Renegotiation between Enron and the Maharashtra government broke down without any progress. After unsuccessful attempts by the company to sell off its entire stake in DPC to either the central government or its lenders, the massive project was ultimately written off. In December 2001, the MNC itself declared bankruptcy and several of its top executives went on trial for malfeasance and extensive off-the-books partnerships worldwide. The moral is clear—procedures for awarding contracts and their evaluation should be as transparent as possible to preclude corruption and rigging.

PORTFOLIO FOREIGN INVESTMENT

In principle PFI is distinguished from DFI by the degree of management control that foreign investors exercise in a project. Portfolio investors provide only financial capital by purchasing shares without any participation in a company's management. (The ownership threshold is somewhat arbitrary. An investment is normally counted as DFI when it involves an equity capital stake of 10 per cent or more). The time horizon is typically much shorter than that of DFI. The type of investors and their motivations are also different. While DFI is usually undertaken by multinational firms, portfolio investors are more often either financial institutions or individuals, or institutional investors such as pension funds, insurance companies, or investment trusts. The primary interest of MNCs is in accessing markets and resources while the overriding motivation for portfolio investors is participation in the profits of local enterprises through capital gains and dividends.

The difference in time horizon and motivations explains why PFI flows are much more volatile than DFI. Over the period 1986–95 the coefficient of variation of global PFI flows was four times that of DFI flows. This volatility is very strongly correlated with the macroeconomic stability of recipient countries.

A look at recent trends in PFI identifies two main recipient regions, Asia and Latin America. Between 1990 and 1993 flows to both regions increased substantially, by more than 500 per cent for Asia and 230 per cent for Latin America. Two major factors have contributed. First, financial liberalization combined with fantastic improvements in communications technology has enabled investors to move their funds quickly between different regions. The prospect of high returns in new and fast growing emerging markets has induced a greater willingness to take risk. Second, the surge in PFI flows to emerging markets has been facilitated by the concentration of enormous financial resources in the hands of institutional investors such as pension funds, insurance companies, and mutual funds in the advanced countries. The identifiable pool of savings with such investors was estimated to be worth US$ 21 trillion in 1993. A sizable portion left for the emerging markets of Asia and Latin America as domestic interest rates (the rate on US Treasury Bill, for example) dropped. There is indeed high correlation between PFI flow and interest rates in developed countries.

INDIA, THE EAST ASIAN CRISIS, AND CAPITAL ACCOUNT CONVERTIBILITY

While it is now much easier for DFI to come into India, international short term borrowing and lending are still subject to many restrictions. This regulatory restraint on short term capital flows has provided effective protection against the type of devastating crisis that hit several East Asian countries in 1997–8 (see also Chapter 5). In all of the five hardest hit countries—Indonesia, South Korea, Malaysia, Thailand, and the Philippines—domestic banks had extremely high exposure to foreign short term debt. Large scale panic ensued when short term reserves dipped below such debt and there was massive and unstoppable outflow of capital triggering the crisis. The Government of India, in contrast, has always kept a very careful eye on the ratio of short term loans from foreign lenders to the country's foreign exchange reserves. This has never gone beyond 30 per cent, unlike in the East Asian crisis countries where it was often greater than 100 per cent.

Currency convertibility means that foreign currencies can be freely obtained from the Central Bank on demand at the prevailing exchange rate. Keeping potentially destabilizing short term speculative capital flows in check necessitates exchange control over asset transactions. This implies absence of full convertibility on capital account. There is pressure on developing countries either to abolish such controls or to loosen them substantially. The Indian rupee is now fully convertible on current account, but capital controls are still firmly in place. Many economists and policy-makers are in favour of drawing a sharp distinction between liberalization of trade in goods and services and the much more questionable case for free movement of capital. Substantial liberalization of capital controls, in their opinion, is sound policy only at a mature stage of economic development. Our government subscribes to this view.

In 1996 a Committee on Capital Account Convertibility was appointed to assess the scope for reform. It recommended a cautious move in a phased manner. Certain essential preconditions were highlighted that include reductions in the rate of inflation and the fiscal deficit and, most importantly, substantial strengthening of the domestic banking system.

FIVE

Exchange Rate, Capital Mobility, and Policy Coordination

The key concepts used in this chapter to analyse the problem of maintaining macrobalance in globalized open economies include the exchange rate, current and capital accounts of BoP, demand and supply of foreign exchange, and speculative flow of capital. The fundamental dilemma of globalization caused by the unstable triad (of pegged exchange, national policy autonomy, and free capital flow) is highlighted. Collapse of the European Monetary System (EMS) and the Asian crisis are discussed and used as telling illustrations. The final section contains a treatment of devaluation as a policy instrument.

The exchange rate, which is the price of one currency in terms of another, is usually quoted as the number of units of the domestic currency required to purchase one unit of foreign currency. Its value, like that of any other price, is determined in the market for foreign exchange by the forces of demand and supply. The value of the exchange rate and changes therein have crucial implications for a nation's returns from international transactions. The returns are encapsulated in the BoP.

A country can finance its imports in three ways: a) exports proceeds, b) interest income on foreign assets, and c) sale of assets (borrowing). If the price of the importable in terms of the exportable is denoted by P, the fundamental relation is:

$$PM = X + C + E \text{ or } (X - PM) + E + C = 0$$

where X = export, M = import, E = net interest payment from abroad (interest received from abroad minus interest paid to foreigners), $C =$ net international sale of assets (total assets sold to foreigners minus those bought from foreigners). X, C, and E are expressed in units of exportables.

> X – PM is the trade balance
> X – PM + E is the current account balance
> C is the capital balance

The current account records all transactions related to income and expenditure in the current period while the capital account records trade in financial assets. Surplus in the capital account implies that net capital inflow is occurring or the economy is borrowing from abroad. This inflow is an addition to the international reserves of the nation.

Perfect capital mobility means that domestic and foreign assets (bonds) are regarded as perfect substitutes by investors, so, to equalize their yields domestic and foreign interest rates must be the same. It assumes a perfectly functioning international capital market and complete absence of national restrictions on movement of capital. At the other extreme of zero capital mobility assets cannot be traded across national borders at all and there is no direct pressure to equalize interest rates. In the intermediate case of imperfect capital mobility bonds can be traded but they are not equivalent. Under capital mobility a rise in the domestic interest rate relative to the foreign rate induces foreigners to buy more of our bonds, implying addition to capital inflow and an improvement in capital balance. There will be an impact on the exchange rate due to the implied change in demand for the domestic currency. This is treated in detail later.

Since a seller or an asset holder is typically interested in returns in terms of his home currency, the exchange rate and expected changes in it will have very important influence on his plans. A Japanese investor's decision of whether to buy a Japanese asset or an Indian asset will depend not only on the interest or rate of return differential, but also on his view of how the exchange rate is going to behave. If the rate fluctuates too much, a disturbing element of uncertainty will come into play to upset the operation of 'real' factors. This is the exchange rate risk of global business. Short term capital flows may contain a speculative element if currency traders expect future exchange rates to differ from the current rates. (A speculator is one who attempts to profit from changes in the exchange rate.) Speculation, of course, may well be of the destabilizing type.

OPEN ECONOMY EQUILIBRIUM

Equilibrium in the simple Keynesian model for an open economy with government requires

$$Y = C + I + G + X - M$$

where the symbols have their standard meaning. P, the relative price of importable, is assumed to be constant. Its value is set equal to unity.

The current account balance (CAB) is:

$$X - M = Y - C - I - G$$

By subtracting and adding taxes T this can be rewritten as

$$CAB = (Y - T - C - I) + (T - G) = (S - I) + (T - G)$$

The first term on the right hand side is the excess of domestic saving over investment and the second term is the budgetary or fiscal surplus.

Suppose for simplicity $T = G$. Then, a surplus in the current account (CAB > 0) implies that savings of domestic residents exceed domestic investment. This excess is invested abroad and represents a net accumulation of foreign assets. Similarly, a current account deficit is a net decumulation of foreign assets. The second term is the excess of taxes over government spending. If the economy's saving is equal to investment a current account deficit (CAB < 0) is associated with a fiscal deficit and a current account surplus with a fiscal surplus.

The open economy equilibrium condition shows clearly that national income will be stimulated by an autonomous rise in exports and adversely affected by a fall. Since the import of a country is the export of its trading partner, it is easy to see how trade can act to transmit business cycles across national boundaries. A recession in one country can trigger a recession in its trade partner by reducing its own imports (the demand for the partner's exports.) Throughout history, this interdependence has been the source of endless trouble in international relations.

Sterilization

Equilibrium in the simple Keynesian model ignores the monetary implications of trade imbalance. A BoP deficit shrinks the monetary base by reducing international reserves and money supply will contract in consequence. This will raise the interest rate which reduces investment and induces capital inflow under capital mobility. The combined effect will be to correct the initial deficit. Thus there is a mechanism (link between BoP and domestic money supply) that ensures that BoP disequilibria are self-correcting under fixed exchange. Loss of control over domestic money supply is, however, entailed. Governments, therefore, often choose to shortcircuit the mechanism by offsetting the impact of BoP deficit or surplus on the monetary base by adopting compensatory policies. This is known as sterilization. Money supply, for example, can be prevented from rising through an open market sale of bonds by the Central Bank or by raising the reserve ratio of commercial banks.

The limit to sterilization will be set by the stock of assets held by the Central Bank. Capital mobility will pose additional problems. Suppose that authorities are selling bonds to offset a BoP surplus. The rate of interest will rise, encouraging capital inflow. This will defeat the purpose of bond sale by increasing the surplus. In the limit, under perfect capital mobility, sterilization becomes impossible even in the short run. In today's world where the efficiency of asset transactions is rising rapidly and national controls on capital movements are being dismantled, maintaining control over money supply in the face of BoP disequilibria is becoming very difficult.

EXCHANGE RATE CONCEPTS

In a multicountry world every currency will have one price against every other currency. Economists usually distinguish between:

(1) Nominal Exchange Rate which is the rate of exchange of any currency in terms of any other. It is thus a bilateral concept.

(2) Effective Exchange Rate which is a weighted average of bilateral rates expressed as an index number relative to some base year. The weights are customarily taken to be the share of the respective countries in the total trade of the country for which the EER is being calculated.

(3) Real Exchange Rate which is designed to measure the rate at which home goods exchange for foreign goods rather than the rate at which currencies themselves are traded. Representing the relative purchasing power of domestic output, it is essentially a measure of international competitiveness.

$$RER = EER \, (P^*/P)$$

where P^* is the foreign currency price of the foreign (imported) good and P the home currency price of the home (exported) good.

A rise in the exchange rate is known as depreciation or devaluation of the home currency. More units of the domestic currency are needed to purchase one unit of foreign currency. (The opposite of devaluation is revaluation.) It is very important to distinguish between a nominal devaluation and a real devaluation.

Suppose, for simplicity, that India trades only with the USA. Let us denote the nominal exchange rate by e (that is, the number of units of rupee needed to obtain one dollar is e). Initially $e = 40$, $P^* = US\$ 4$, $P = Rs 10$, so that RER = 16. After a 10 per cent devaluation of the rupee, $e = 44$. If there is no change in the price ratio for the two countries RER will be proportional to e and RER also will rise exactly by 10 per cent—a real devaluation of 10 per cent. But if along with the change in the nominal rate, P also rises by 10 per cent relative to P^* nominal devaluation will fail to generate a real devaluation. For a real devaluation to take place nominal devaluation must not be offset by a rise in domestic inflation relative to inflation in the foreign trading partner. Thus:

Proportional change in RER = Proportional change in nominal exchange minus the excess of domestic inflation over foreign inflation (inflation differential).

A currency is said to maintain purchasing power parity if it depreciates by an amount equal to the excess of domestic inflation over foreign inflation. In this case RER will stay unchanged. The purchasing power parity principle states that movements in exchange rates reflect differences in relative inflation rates across countries. If prices rise in one country relative to another, exchange rate will adjust upwards (depreciate) to compensate. Empirical evidence on the issue is mixed. It does reveal positive correlation between movements in exchange rates and inflation rates, but the correlation, contrary to the prediction of the theory, is far from perfect.

EXCHANGE RATE DETERMINATION

As mentioned earlier, the exchange rate is determined by supply and demand in the foreign exchange market. Indian companies wishing to import goods will sell rupee to buy foreign currencies with which to pay the suppliers abroad, tourists visiting India sell their own currencies to buy rupee, if a British company intends to buy a bond issued by the Government of India or to buy a factory in Gujarat, it will convert pound sterling into rupee. An Indian bank wishing to make a sterling deposit in London will sell rupee to buy sterling. Thus demand for foreign exchange arises as a result of import of goods and services and outflow of capital—purchase of plants and equipment overseas (DFI) or acquisition of overseas bonds and securities by domestic asset holders (PFI). Supply is created by exports of goods and services and inflow of capital. In other words, each debit item in BoP represents a demand for foreign currency and each credit item a supply.

Other things remaining unchanged, the demand for rupee increases when the exchange rate rises (the price of rupee falls) as the price of Indian goods to consumers abroad fall in their own currencies, increasing the demand for India's exports. The supply of rupee, on the other hand, normally goes down as the price of rupee falls because foreign goods become more expensive in rupee in our own market, thereby reducing our import demand. Thus demand and supply curves for rupee have their normal shape when plotted against the price of rupee (inverse of the exchange rate).The determination of the exchange rate (the price of rupee) is shown in Figure 5.1.

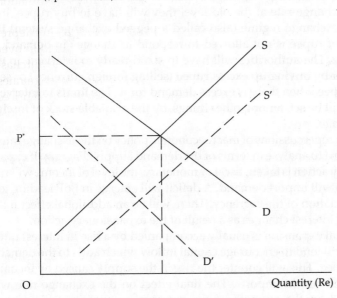

Figure 5.1: Exchange Rate Determination

A deficit in the balance of trade (BoT) (imports exceeding exports) implies that supply of rupee will exceed demand and the price of rupee will tend to fall to reach its equilibrium level. This will be allowed to happen in a floating exchange regime, but in a fixed or managed system the overvalued rate can be supported only by buying up the excess rupee in exchange for foreign exchange. The reverse is true when the trade balance is in surplus.

Although the price level of the country does not appear explicitly in the figure, it can be used to analyse the effect of price changes. Suppose P rises relative to P'. This will induce a general substitution in favour of foreign goods and away from home goods. The induced rise in import demand will shift the supply curve to the right and the equilibrium price of rupee will fall, as predicted by purchasing power parity.

Demand and supply curves can shift for a number of reasons. A change in taste and preference for foreign goods will cause a rightward shift in supply, a leftward shift in demand might be due to a fall in the rate of interest in India as investors switch their funds out of the Indian money market. In either case the equilibrium price of rupee will fall implying a depreciation. This would be the outcome under a flexible or floating exchange system. If the authorities wish to keep the exchange rate at the old level they will have to buy rupee. In a fixed exchange regime (also called a pegged exchange system) the price of rupee is not allowed to respond to changes in demand or supply. The authorities will have to stand ready to intervene in the market by buying up excess rupee (selling foreign currency) or selling rupee when there is excess demand for it. The limits to intervention will be set, among other things, by the available stock of foreign exchange.

The repercussions of macroeconomic policy on the exchange rate is not hard to analyse in terms of the demand supply diagram. If expansionary action is taken, fiscal or monetary, the level of income will rise and so will import demand. A deficit will emerge in BoP leading to a depreciation of the currency. There will be an additional effect if the rate of interest changes as a result of the expansionary action.

Fiscal expansion is usually accompanied by a rise in interest rates. This will tend to encourage capital inflow which adds to the demand for rupee. This will counter the rise in the supply caused by income-induced rise in imports. The final effect on the exchange rate will depend on the strength of the marginal propensity to import in relation to the elasticity of capital flows. For a monetary expansion, income rises but interest rate falls. Supply of rupee goes up on both counts and rupee's price falls unambiguously.

In the late 1970s the USA used monetary policy mainly to promote recovery and the dollar depreciated. In the early 1980s, in contrast, reliance was mainly on fiscal policy. Budget deficit was accompanied by a rise in interest rate, inducing a large inflow of capital and the dollar appreciated sharply. Canada has traditionally shown a preference for tight monetary policy to keep inflation in check. This kept the interest rate high and resulted in a strong Canadian dollar. This has hurt exporters and reduced Canada's gains from trade with the USA and Mexico. Interestingly, public opinion has tended to overlook the role of monetary policy and put most of the blame for rising unemployment on the reduction in trade barriers.

The demand and supply curves for rupee (and, therefore, the value of the rupee) in Figure 5.1 respond not only to domestic policies but to macropolicies of our trading partners as well. Suppose, the USA raises its rate of interest as part of a contractionary monetary policy US bonds become more attractive to Indian investors and, as a result, capital flows out, causing a downward pressure on rupee (upward pressure on dollar). This pressure can be relieved by raising the interest rate in India, but the result may be an economic recession with declining employment. If, instead, the USA had stimulated domestic spending by tax cuts or expansion in money supply, its imports from India would have gone up, exerting an upward pressure on the rupee.

This interlinkage of domestic policies and national exchange rates has given rise to what has aptly been termed an unstable triumvirate: pegged or managed exchange rates, autonomous macropolicies and extensive capital flows. This can be summarized as:

The Fundamental Dilemma of Globalization

To reduce the exchange rate risk of doing global business, purchase and sale of goods and services as well as assets, a managed system of relatively fixed exchange is needed, but this is difficult to achieve without international policy coordination (loss of national autonomy) and/or restrictions on capital movements (curb on globalization).

Since a return to capital controls goes fundamentally against the spirit of globalization, all sorts of debates and discussions are going on to facilitate better policy harmonization among the partners in the liberalized world trading order. Rather than becoming part of a multilateral trading order, like-minded nations with similar economic

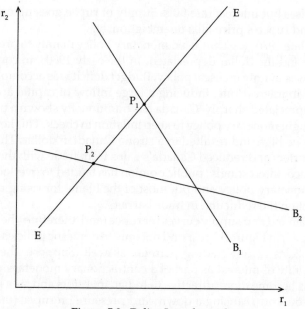

Figure 5.2: Policy Interdependence

structures are favouring the formation of regional blocs because that would make policy coordination easier.

Policy interdependence and the need for coordination can be illustrated in a simple model. Consider two countries operating under a pegged exchange rate. Each has a single instrument, the interest rate, to achieve two objectives, internal and external balance.

The curve B_1 in the diagram shows the interest rate combinations that permit Country 1 to attain internal balance. The two rates are denoted by r_1 and r_2. If r_2 rises, investment, income, and imports of Country 2 will fall. To counter the effect of falling export on its income Country 1 must reduce r_1. The curve B_2 shows the combinations that maintain internal balance in Country 2. B_1 is steeper than B_2 on the reasonable assumption that a change in a country's own rate of interest affects its income more strongly than an equal change in its trade partner. The curve EE plots the interest rate combinations that preserve external balance between the countries. If Country 2 reduces its imports and attracts inflow of capital by raising its interest rate, Country 1 will be forced to do the same to restore its external balance. The optimum point for Country 1 is P_1 while that for Country 2 is P_2. This incompatibility of national aims makes coordination necessary.

BOX 5.1: Collapse of the European Monetary System

Collapse of the EMS provides a very illuminating illustration of the difficulties of maintaining a system of managed exchange rates in the present era of deregulation and global integration. Established in 1978, the core of EMS was an agreement to maintain currencies within a 2.25 per cent band of a fixed rate against the ecu, a currency composite created for official transactions within the EU. (see Chapter 6 for a brief history of the EU). The hegemonic financial power of Germany with a traditionally conservative Bundesbank controlling the supply of the reserve currency deutschemark, played a key role in sustaining the agreement.

Until the full liberalization of financial markets in the EU in 1992, a number of member countries with weaker currencies continued to maintain capital controls. Italy, for example, could afford to follow lax macropolicies by restricting capital outflow to a stronger German currency. Some devaluations and revaluations outside the band also did occur, but not with high frequency.

After liberalization speculators and currency traders with their advanced technical equipment moved in on a big scale. When particular currencies came under serious pressure action was taken to realign the fixed rates. But the threat of destabilizing speculation constantly hovered in the background. The final blow was struck by German unification. The huge expenditure needed to finance the unification was mostly raised through borrowing, as the German Chancellor had ruled against taxation. The German interest rate went up to unprecedented heights. With capital controls removed, other European countries faced extreme pressure on their currencies. They were unwilling to match the German interest rate because that would worsen the recession in their economies. Revaluation of the German mark as a possible solution, favoured by the Bundesbank, was once again rejected by the Chancellor on the ground that it would lead to a decline in exports and loss of jobs. Bereft of capital controls, governments found it increasingly difficult to maintain the band in the face of rampant speculation. After spending astronomical amounts in unsuccessful interventions several countries, including the UK, finally left the Exchange Rate Mechanism of the EMS in September 1992.

Source: Ethier (1995), Kenen (2000).

SPECULATION, CAPITAL MOBILITY, AND ECONOMIC STABILITY

Under a freely floating or fully flexible exchange rate the price of a country's currency may be subject to wide and very frequent fluctuations, reflecting changes not only in 'real' trade flows (flow of goods and services in exports and imports) but also in financial flows involved in arbitrage, hedging, and pure speculation. This fluctuation is likely to prove very disruptive for business activities by exposing traders to serious currency risks. Moreover, since future expectations are heavily influenced by the volatility of current prices, the risk of the market becoming disorderly and unstable becomes unbearably high. A fixed exchange regime, in contrast, guarantees that trade can proceed at a given parity against one or more other major currencies. That guarantee comes from the Central Bank that uses open market interventions to keep the rate constant (or within a narrow band) by purchasing the home currency if its value is falling, or selling it if it is rising.

The best example of a long term fixed exchange arrangement was the Bretton Woods System, which lasted for almost thirty years before collapsing in 1973. Every participating country had to peg its currency to gold or to the US dollar. The USA in turn pegged the dollar to gold, at the rate of US$ 35 per ounce. In addition all countries were asked to do away with exchange controls and to make their currencies fully convertible. They were expected to intervene to keep their rates within a narrow band of their pegs while at the same time directing domestic policies toward maintaining desirable macroeconomic conditions. In case a country found that its BoP was in 'fundamental disequilibrium' (a term that was never defined) it was permitted to adjust its peg after obtaining the approval of the newly created IMF. Thus it was supposed to be an adjustable peg system, a compromise between fully fixed and floating rates.

The system of adjustable pegs lasted until the end of the 1960s without any substantial hitch, although a major realignment occurred in 1949 when sterling was devalued. The pound was devalued again in 1967 while France devalued its currency in 1969. On the issue of convertibility it was unrealistic to expect countries to promptly eliminate all war-time exchange controls and other restrictions on convertibility. It was not until the beginning of the 1960s that most industrial nations had restored current account convertibility.

In the post-war years as the European economies and Japan began to recover, the huge US trade surplus started to decline while outflow of dollar due to foreign aid and investment continued to increase. By 1960 the USA no longer had sufficient gold reserves to back all the dollar holdings abroad and for the first time there was a crisis of confidence in the dollar. The US administration, however, refused either to devalue the dollar or to pursue a contractionary policy at home to reduce the payments deficit. At the same time Germany and Japan did not want to revalue their currencies as that would impact adversely on exports. Finally, in 1971 the Nixon administration froze prices and wages to combat inflation and closed the Treasury's Gold Window in an attempt to force a new realignment of the pegged rates. This proved futile and the System collapsed in 1973. Since then exchange rates have mostly floated under control and the IMF has abolished the obligation to peg currencies to gold. It continues, however, to closely monitor the performance of its member countries and intervenes whenever a country asks for assistance to fight serious and persistent BoP problems.

Today's capital markets are characterized by huge speculative and hedging flows over which national governments have very little control. As a consequence, any programme of maintaining fixed currency values is extremely difficult to maintain. This is dramatically illustrated by Britain's exit from the European Exchange Rate Mechanism (ERM). On the day sterling was forced to withdraw from the ERM (16 September 1992) Bank of England spent an estimated £ 7 billion, roughly a third of its foreign exchange reserve, in buying sterling with deutschemarks in an attempt to preserve sterling exchange within the permitted ERM band. Not surprisingly, most currencies (including the rupee) are now allowed to float more or less freely under 'dirty float', where Central Banks try to iron out the biggest fluctuations on a day-to-day basis but make no attempt to maintain a long term rate.

The globalization of finance markets in recent years has been nothing short of revolutionary. The days are all but gone when national authorities could stabilize financial markets through banking regulations, limits on interest rates and separation of commercial and investment banking. Advances in IT and data processing have transformed global operation to the point where US$ 1.5 trillion is transferred every day around the world. This is many times the annual value of world trade in goods. (In 1990 commercial banks in the USA spent US$ 15 billion on IT alone.) The cost of operation has come down so drastically that a multimillion dollar transfer across the globe can be accomplished for just 18 US cents. Most of these high speed electronic transactions are almost impossible to trace, let alone regulate. The implication is clear. Governments are left nearly powerless to ensure stable and orderly financial markets.

The tremendous acceleration in speculation encouraged by wideranging financial deregulation and aided by the revolution in communications technology has inevitably precipitated several crises within the past few years. One near melt-down occurred in 1995 when news spread around the world that Mexico was on the verge of defaulting on its enormous debt. Immediately capital took flight from a very large number of stock markets around the globe. The situation was saved at the last moment when the US government stepped in to bail out Mexico (or rather its own investors in Mexico).

Just two-and-half years later, in mid-1997, a similar panic spread across East Asia. This time the crisis began in Thailand but quickly moved to neighbouring regions. In country after country 'hot money' left at lightning speed. Big time speculators like George Soros deepened the chaos by betting against the currencies in trouble. Currencies and stock markets crashed, spreading dislocation and ruin. Let us take a closer look at the phenomenon.

The Asian Crisis

In the quarter century preceding 1997 East Asian economies of Singapore, Hong Kong, South Korea, and Taiwan made their transition from low cost manufacturing centres to high value-added service economies. The annual average growth in GDP for these countries in real terms was around 10 per cent over the period. Other Asian economies such as China, Indonesia, Malaysia, and Thailand gradually emerged as new low cost manufacturing centres for western and Japanese MNCs.

Most of these NICs (newly industrializing countries) had made currencies completely convertible by removing all exchange controls and had pegged their currencies to the dollar. Foreign credit expanded wildly as investors perceived little or no currency risk and the interest rate was high. A part of the short term credit was required to be kept in liquid form and this was invested in US Treasury Bills. The interest rate on the Bills being fairly low, it was a very palatable arrangement for the USA. While a substantial amount of the huge inflow of short term credit was used for genuinely productive purposes, a growing percentage was finding its way into speculation, particularly in real estate. Under imperfect screening and poor supervision, banks and finance companies in Thailand borrowed dollar and yen freely from foreign banks (often without covering their exposure in the forward market) and granted loans to dubious borrowers for projects with low economic viability. A major Thai bank had failed a full year ahead of the crisis. This set foreign investors, but not the government, worrying about the fragility of the banking system.

Slowdown in western economies and a deep recession in Japan accompanied by a falling yen triggered the crisis through a sharp reduction in exports from the region. Under a floating rate this would have led to a sharp fall in the value of domestic currencies, but the authorities tried to maintain the pegged rates by intervening in the market. It became apparent that such intervention could not last long. Expectation of significant devaluation opened the floodgate to the sale of local currencies and short term credit took flight. The boom in residential and commercial construction, fed by unrealistic expectations, also collapsed.

On 2 July 1997 Thailand devalued the baht. That led to a downward spiral that quickly spread to the other economies, because the countries trade heavily with one another. Devaluation, speculative attack on currencies, and flight from them became the norm. Steep depreciation of local currencies had a shattering impact on banks and companies burdened by huge foreign currency debts. Growth rates became zero or negative for most of the 'tigers'.

The IMF moved in to shore up Indonesia, Korea, and Thailand with its standard formula of tight fiscal and monetary policies to preserve exchange rates and government solvency. The result was to turn the crisis into a deep recession. There were widespread unrest and violence everywhere, particularly in Indonesia. When recovery did become discernible in some economies this was generally regarded as coming in spite of, rather than because of, the IMF. To be fair to the Fund it should be pointed out that back in 1996 it had warned Thailand that the budget deficit was too high (8 per cent of GDP) and advised caution in the conduct of monetary and trade policy. This was repeated in early 1997, but was ignored again by the government.

It is becoming clear that in a world where the bulk of foreign exchange transactions is not accounted for by payments for traded goods, sustaining a viable system of managed rates will require a reimposition of exchange controls, at least on the capital account. Although that will entail a retreat from the globalization of capital markets, a very serious threat to a stable order of liberal trade will be countered thereby.

The lesson from the Asian crisis for the LDCs is simple and clear. There should be no hurry in dismantling capital controls and the domestic financial sector should be under strict supervision. The Basle Committee on Banking Supervision set out some core principles in 1997 to improve supervision of banks. They relate to licensing, prudential regulation, and principles of multinational banking. India has accepted most of the recommendations.

DEVALUATION

A deliberate reduction in the price of the home currency (under a fixed or managed exchange rate) is known as devaluation. What is the likely impact on the BoP? For simplicity, let us assume there are no capital transactions, so that BoP and BoT are the same.

The BoT surplus, measured in home currency, can be written as:

$$B = PX - eP^* M$$

Suppose that all prices are held fixed in terms of the seller's currency, that is, P and P^* do not change following a devaluation (a rise in e).

Under this condition it is easy to show that devaluation will improve the trade balance if the sum of the elasticities of import demand of the two countries exceed unity. This condition, written usually as $(e + e^* > 1)$, is known as the Marshall–Lerner condition. (Note that the symbol e here denotes elasticities of respective import demands, not the exchange rate.) The chief message is that devaluation will not work if demand elasticities are low.

Even if elasticities are high enough the immediate impact of devaluation on the BoT may be adverse. This is because some time must pass before changes in exchange rate can translate into changes in price and then demand takes some time to change in response to the change in price. Therefore, trade balance may trace a J-shaped curve through time—first declining and then rising—in the wake of a devaluation. This J-curve effect is a very widely observed phenomenon.

One reason why many countries are reluctant to make use of devaluation to improve trade balance is that there is a direct relationship between devaluation and domestic inflation. This is because cost of imports enter significantly into the retail price index. The rise in the prices of imported fuel and other intermediate industrial inputs will be passed on to the consumers, particularly for the commodities for which market power of the seller is high. As the cost of living rises workers will start demanding higher wages to protect their real income. This will lead to another round of price escalation.

To summarize, the final impact of a devaluation on consumer prices will depend on: (a) the import content of production, (b) the extent to which cost increases can be passed on to consumers, (c) the import content of consumption, and (d) the sensitivity of wage demands to escalations in cost of living.

Another problem is that although a single country may improve its export prospects by devaluation, the effect may vanish if its rivals also follow suit. Under competitive devaluation there is no change in relative position of the exporting countries, while the importing nations benefit from the reduction in price. The exporters suffer the adverse effects without any compensating gain from currency depreciation. This Prisoners' Dilemma-type situation was very much evident in East Asia.

A country with an overvalued exchange rate or undervalued currency (relative to the equilibrium, so that there is a trade surplus) may be reluctant to revalue, because that will entail recession through fall in exports and rise in imports. A further important concern is liquidity. If demand elasticities are low then exchange rate changes may not work, and even under high elasticities the downward portion of the J-curve may turn out to be too long. Until the adjustment takes place the country running a deficit will have to draw down its international reserves of foreign exchange or gold, assuming borrowing is not possible. Where liquidity is thin, disequilibrium in the payments balance inevitably leads to restrictions on imports or on convertibility of currency (exchange controls).

The policy of import-substituting industrialization, now largely abandoned by most LDCs, involved numerous and ever proliferating measures to curb imports of manufactures. Thus the demand for foreign exchange (supply of domestic currency) was artificially restricted leading to an overvaluation of the currency relative to its market clearing level. This reduced the competitiveness of exporters. In its determined effort to turn LDCs away from import substitution to export promotion, the IMF puts relentless pressure for currency devaluation. At the same time to make devaluation real and not nominal it also urges cut in the fiscal deficit to contain inflationary pressures. Devaluation with a view to bringing the exchange rate closer to its equilibrium value in tandem with fiscal prudence forms the core of the IMF's stabilization package. Under no circumstances

BOX 5.2: India's Exchange Rate Policy

As an important step towards economic reform, the rupee was devalued in July 1991 by 24 per cent and a dual exchange rate was introduced in March 1992. Next year the rates were unified which was allowed to float. Between June 1991 and March 1993 there was a 35 per cent depreciation relative to the dollar. It was a real devaluation of around 27 per cent vis-à-vis our major trading rivals. This undoubtedly gave a boost to exports.

The RBI continues to intervene periodically to maintain orderly conditions in the foreign exchange market. Although there is no explicit real exchange target, the RER has shown remarkable stability in recent years. With the 1985 level as 100, the 5-country index has settled around a value of 52–53 per cent since 1992.

Full convertibility of the rupee on current account was announced in 1994. However, the capital account continues to be under careful regulation, insulating the exchange rate against the capricious influx and outflow of short term capital.

are capital and exchange controls looked upon with favour. Obstinate enforcement of this orthodoxy when an economy is already in deep recession with high unemployment and is facing speculative attack on its currency can only be described as treatment worse than the disease. That it can be seriously counterproductive was conclusively shown during the crisis in East Asia.

SIX

Free Trade, Protectionism, and Regional Trading Blocs

In the post-war years there was phenomenal expansion of international trade and commerce. The sustained prosperity of the USA and the spectacular recovery of Western Europe and Japan would not have materialized without the abundant flow of goods, services, and technical knowledge across national boundaries. Free trade indeed acted as a powerful engine of growth, at least among the industrial countries. During the 1960s the Asian economies of South Korea, Hong Kong, Singapore, and Taiwan made strategic use of foreign trade policy to launch their economies on a path of sustained growth and industrialization. Their standard of living rapidly approached that of their more affluent trading partners. Strategic use of trade instruments involved creation of maximum incentives for exports, while maintaining barriers to trade and other types of control in some other areas. So it was not a matter of free trade out and out.

This chapter aims to present the basic case for unrestricted trade from the economic point of view and at the same time acquaint the reader with the multifarious tools that have been used by nations to restrict international trade for economic and non-economic objectives. The celebrated infant industry argument for protection is subjected to scrutiny. An account of the evolution of the global order of multilateral, non-discriminatory trading under GATT over the last half-century is included to provide the institutional background. The formation of regional trading blocs (RTB) has been an important parallel development, partially nullifying the programme of GATT. The economics of RTBs is presented in simple terms. Unable to capture all aspects of this complex phenomenon, this chapter succeeds nonetheless in giving the essential idea. It concludes with a brief history of the EU, the most successful case of economic integration to date.

BENEFIT OF FREE TRADE

International exchange is welfare-improving because it gives a country the opportunity to devote its scarce resources to the production of those goods where its relative efficiency is greatest. The country is said to have a comparative advantage in such goods. Part of the outputs can be exchanged to obtain imports at cost lower than that of domestic production. The relocation of resources in each trading country according to principle of comparative advantage would raise total world output above the level it would achieve in the absence of trade, with the gains shared via exchange between the countries. Adam Smith's principle of division of labour is extended to a global scale. The degree of the gains from trade to any country would depend on the terms of trade, that is, the ratio of export to import prices. Other things being equal the higher the terms of trade the greater is the benefit.

The benefit of trade is illustrated in Figure 6.1. In the absence of trade, domestic price of the product of the industry (call it industry X) is P_1. The industry structure is assumed to be competitive. Social welfare W = Consumers' Surplus (CS) + Producers' Surplus (PS) is the area AEB. If the world price of the good P_w is below P_1 (a case of comparative disadvantage) the country will be better off importing the good. In free trade domestic price will be forced down to P_w. Total domestic demand at this price is Q_2, which will be met by domestic supply Q_1 and import $Q_1 Q_2$. CS has increased from AP_1E to $A P_w G$ and PS has fallen from $BP_1 E$ to $BP_w F$, giving a net gain in welfare of area C. The losers (the producers) can be compensated by the gainers (the consumers). It is also clear that the gain is positively related to the gap between P_1 and P_w.

As domestic production shrinks from the pre-trade level workers will be laid off, but our welfare function does not attach any separate weight to this loss. Defenders of free trade argue that the loss of employment in the import competing sectors will be offset by the expansion of the export sectors where the country has comparative advantage. But the major problems with this line of reasoning are: (a) the expanding industries may have no need for the type of labour that is thrown out of the contracting ones, and (b) even if the worker does

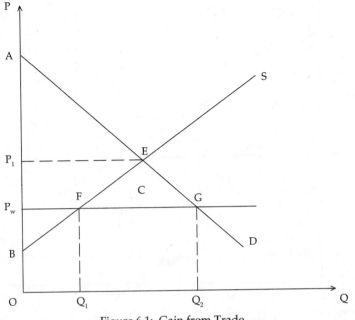

Figure 6.1: Gain from Trade

find a job the cost of moving to the new place of work may be very high or even prohibitive. Think of a person who loses a job in West Bengal and succeeds in finding a willing employer in Tamil Nadu or Rajasthan or Gujarat. By not paying sufficient attention to these costs advocates of liberalization fail to make their case convincing to the man in the street.

It should be kept in mind that Figure 6.1 is based on a partial equilibrium analysis of free trade for an industry. Secondary effects of trade on factor markets, on the terms of trade, or on the BoP and the exchange rate are not considered. If the industry in question has considerable weight in the national economy these secondary effects will be important. The demand and supply curves in the graph will not stay put after the opening up of trade. Full general equilibrium analysis will be needed. The implicit assumption behind the figure is that the industry is a small part of the country's economy and the country is a small player in the international market for the product.

Figure 6.2 shows the gain from trade when the industry X is controlled by a monopolist. In the situation before trade the price is P_m and quantity Q_m. When trade is opened up the world price P_w acts as

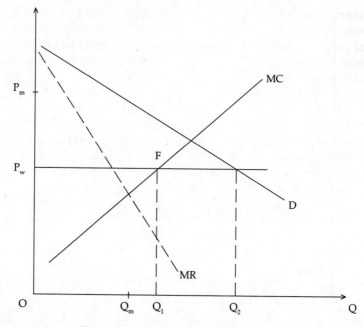

Figure 6.2: Monopoly under Free Trade

a price ceiling for the seller. His equilibrium shifts to F, where domestic supply is Q_1 and import equals $Q_1 Q_2$. Welfare is higher as the industry has moved closer to the optimal point (where $P = MC$). Free trade reduces monopoly power by introducing competition. This pro-competitive aspect will be an additional source of gain if it reduces or eliminates X-inefficiency by forcing the seller to go for cost cutting measures.

The new trade theory of international exchange of differentiated products (developed by Avinash Dixit, Paul Krugman, and others) has added a major new element to the possible gains from free trade. The central element of this approach is the recognition of the importance of variety or product differentiation both for consumption and production. Consumers derive greater utility from a wider menu of choice and the onset of diminishing returns in production can be successfully countered by introducing newer types of inputs. Trade in differentiated products and inputs subject to scale economies becomes beneficial even between otherwise identical partners. This has important implication for the policy of protection in LDCs. Their markets being small, these economies in isolation are able to accommodate only a narrow range of variety of products as well as inputs. By radically widening the range of choice (to consumers of final goods as well as to entrepreneurs with respect to inputs and techniques) international trade has the potential to confer substantial welfare gain.

A very intriguing point of international interdependence is that although free trade is beneficial for all countries taken together, unilateral movement towards it may not be desirable. This is another instance of the Prisoners' Dilemma. Consider a world of only two countries where each has two policy options (strategies)—free trade (FT), or protection (P). Consider the hypothetical payoff matrix (where the first entry in each cell is the gain or payoff to Country 1).

		Country 2	
		FT	P
Country 1	FT	15, 15	−10, 20
	P	20, −10	−5, −5

It is easy to check that protection is the dominant strategy of each nation, leading them to the lower right hand cell. (If Country 1 chooses FT then P is better for Country 2 because 20 > 15, and if Country 1 chooses P even then P is better for 2 because (−5) > (−10). Thus P is the dominant strategy for 2. The situation is exactly similar for Country 1.) Free trade would have been better for both, but the upper left cell will not be the outcome of free choice. Intervention of a third party is needed to coax a coordinated choice of FT and to ensure that the parties stick to that choice subsequently and do not revert to their dominant strategy of protection. This provides a justification for supranational coordinating bodies like the World Trade Organization (WTO).

In recent years there has been a surge across the globe towards a regime of free trade. The chief architect of this triumph is the celebrated General Agreement on Tariffs and Trade (GATT).

A BRIEF HISTORY OF GATT: (1947–94)

The years following World War I witnessed a retreat from relatively unrestricted trade into intense protectionism. US tariffs (import duties) reached their peak with the Hawley–Smoot Tariff of 1930. During the depression years countries created high trade barriers to protect employment in their own economies. Trade liberalization began again with President Roosevelt's Trade Agreements Programme. The process was interrupted by World War II, to be resumed in 1944 when policy-makers from the UK and the USA met in Bretton Woods, New Hampshire, USA, to lay the foundation for a cooperative international economic order following the war. The Bretton Woods Agreement envisaged the creation of three key international institutions: a) the International Monetary Fund (IMF), b) the International Bank for Reconstruction and Development (IBRD), commonly known as the World Bank, and c) the International Trade Organization, whose task was to oversee the negotiation and administration of a new, multilateral, liberal world trading regime.

After the war the IMF and the World Bank were duly created, but the ITO was aborted because the Havana Charter that would have created it was not approved by the US Congress. Instead, a provisional agreement among twenty-three major trading nations, the GATT, started functioning from 1947 as the institutional framework for global trade liberalization.

Under the GATT some eight negotiating rounds have now been successfully concluded, the latest (the Uruguay Round) involving 130 participants was concluded in December 1993. These negotiations focussed on reciprocal concessions and were very successful in achieving reduction in average world tariffs on manufactured goods. The average rate has come down from 40 per cent in 1947 to 5 per cent today. In the initial phase the most serious impediment was the 'peril point' principle which forbade American negotiators from cutting tariffs below levels at which domestic producers would suffer material injury.

The US Trade Expansion Act of 1962 abolished the peril point. A provision for trade adjustment assistance to be given directly to companies and workers was substituted and paved the way for the Kennedy Round (1964–7) of multilateral trade negotiations. As a result of this round tariffs on imports of industrial goods by GATT signatories fell by over a third between 1967 and 1972. Against this huge gain on the industrial front must be set the decision by the European Economic Community (EEC) to develop a highly protectionist Common Agricultural Policy (CAP) (discussed later). CAP was adopted in 1968. The Tokyo Round (1973–9), while continuing the process of across-the-board tariff cuts on manufactures, for the first time directed serious attention to various non-tariff barriers (NTB) to trade. Codes of conduct were agreed upon in various areas—

customs valuation procedures, government procurement, regulations relating to health, safety, and the environment, subsidies, and dumping. Tariff cut of 38 per cent was achieved for trade between the DCs, while a smaller reduction, 25 per cent, was agreed for trade between the DCs and the LDCs.

Protectionist pressures built up strongly in the 1970s and became more intense in the early 1980s in the wake of the worldwide recession caused by the oil shocks. The emergence of the NICs such as Brazil, South Korea, Singapore, Taiwan, and Hong Kong as major competitive forces in industrial goods, induced industries (and labour unions) in the advanced countries to seek more protection. A phase of new protectionism began to emerge in the 1970s with countries increasingly resorting to trade barriers other than tariffs, industrial and agricultural subsidies, and antidumping or countervailing duties. The boom of the 1960s had witnessed a rapid growth of export of textiles and clothing from the developing countries. Protectionist forces succeeded in converting the Long Term Arrangement on Cotton Textiles (LTA) of 1962 into the much more stringent Multifibre Arrangement (MFA), which permitted advanced countries to impose quantitative restrictions on imports of both natural and synthetic textile and clothing. By the late 1980s MFA encompassed thousands of bilateral product-specific quotas, a blatant violation of the central non-discrimination principle of GATT. Naturally, intense resentment built up among the LDCs, for whom such exports, drawing on large pools of semiskilled and unskilled labour, promised to be an important means of sharing the fruits of global prosperity. MFA is discussed in Chapter 7.

A number of provisions in GATT allowed deviation from its programme of progressive dismantling of barriers to trade. Article 6 permitted retaliation for 'dumping', if it could be proved. Article 18 provided 'escape clauses' to LDCs to protect their infant industries and BoP. According to Article 19 tariff cut could be postponed if rising imports seriously threatened domestic production.

In addition to trade liberalization, non-discrimination was the second fundamental principle championed by GATT. The chief instrument for achieving this was the most favoured nation clause (MFN). MFN requires that any favourable treatment given by a country to any other must be accorded to all the countries that have MFN status with it. Thus if a group of countries sign a treaty containing the MFN clause no other country can get a more favourable treatment from any of them. Bilateral agreements automatically have multilateral

---

BOX 6.1: From GATT to WTO: A chronology

1947: Twenty-three countries sign the GATT in Geneva.

1948: ITO Charter (Havana Charter) drafted. India acceeds to GATT.

1949: Annecy Round of negotiations, eleven nations participate.

1950: China withdraws from GATT. ITO fails to be ratified by the US Congress (Torquay Round).

1951: West Germany joins GATT.

1955: The USA is granted waiver for certain agricultural policies. Japan joins.

1956: Fourth round held in Geneva.

1957: Treaty of Rome creates the European Economic Community.

1960: Dillon Round is started and concluded in 1961.

1962: The Long Term Agreement on Cotton Textile is negotiated.

1964: Kennedy Round begins (concluded in 1967). UNCTAD is created to be a forum for the LDCs.

1965: Par IV, 'On Trade and Development' is added to GATT setting out guidelines for policies towards LDCs.

1973: Tokyo Round is initiated (concluded in 1979).

1974: MFA enters into force. It is renegotiated in 1977, 1982, and extended in 1986, 1991, 1992.

1986: Launching of the Uruguay Round. Mexico joins GATT.

1988: A ministerial meeting to review progress is held in Montreal.

1990: Canada formally introduces a proposal to create an international organization to oversee GATT, the General Agreement on Trade and Services (GATS), and other agreements reached in the Uruguay Round.

1994: On 15 April the Final Act is signed in Marrakesh, establishing the WTO and embodying the results of the Uruguay Round.

1995: From 1 January the WTO starts functioning. (China becomes a member of the WTO in December 2001).

---

consequences. MFN was not GATT's invention. It played a crucial role in European movements towards free trade in the previous century. For example, because of MFN France had to give the German customs union, Zollverein, the concessions it had given Britain under the Cobden–Chevalier Treaty of 1860. When, under the US–UK trade agreement of 1938, there was a reduction in duty on imports from the

UK, duties were also simultaneously reduced on imports from France, the Soviet Union, and Ireland because of the MFN clause. (On numerous occasions countries have sought to evade MFN by adopting very narrow definitions of commodities in tariff legislation. The most dramatic example is provided by German tariff law of 1902 which, in order to prevent Denmark from enjoying the benefits of tariff concessions given to Swiss cattle, defined a distinct commodity: 'brown or dappled cows reared at a level of at least 300 metres above sea level and passing at least one month in every summer at an altitude of at least 800 metres'.) Exceptions to MFN are allowed by GATT in special cases, such as the creation of a free trade area or customs union (Article 24).

The most recent GATT round is known as the Uruguay Round, because the preliminary meeting was held in 1986 in Punta del Este of Uruguay.

Major Issues of Multilateral Trade Negotiations of the Uruguay Round

Trade in agricultural goods

Although agriculture accounts for a substantial proportion of world trade (currently it is 12 per cent), strong farm lobbies have succeeded in the past in keeping agriculture out of GATT-sponsored multilateral trade negotiations. At last it could be included in the agenda of the Uruguay Round. The USA and other exporters of agricultural goods took a very aggressive position against the extremely protectionist CAP of the EU. (The European Economic Community (EEC), became the European Union after the Maastricht Treaty of 1991. To avoid confusion we will, however, use the term EU to discuss events even before the Maastricht Treaty. See 'History of the EU' which is discussed later in this chapter). Over time CAP has developed into a complex web of sales and price guarantees, subsidies, and other measures to keep farmers' income insulated from the forces of global competition in the member countries. For most agricultural products high minimum prices were set for sale in EU markets. This called for a drastic restriction of imports, which was achieved by variable import levies—duties on imported goods determined by the gap between world price and the support price. Thus whatever cost advantage a foreign supplier might enjoy was completely neutralized. This, combined with the fact that the minimum price was fixed so that the least efficient union producer could make a profit, ensured huge rents for the more efficient farmers. The high support price naturally resulted in a surplus of production over domestic demand. This surplus continued to rise over time. To keep price from coming down under the pressure of excess supply governments paid export subsidies to farmers so that the surplus could be disposed of in foreign markets. Over the post-war period the CAP has transformed, at high cost, the EU from the world's largest importer of temperate zone agricultural products to the world's second largest exporter. The USA and other exporters have been seriously hit. New Zealand, for example, experienced the double shock of vanishing EU demand for butter coupled with increased subsidy-aided competition in third markets as the EU started unloading its enormous stockpile (This is the famous butter mountain. There was also a wine lake.)

In addition to being enormously complex (it uses twenty different systems of prices) CAP is extremely costly both in terms of consumers' welfare and as a drain on the budgetary resources of governments. However, the EU is not the only player of this game. Japan's markets for many agricultural products, rice in particular, was one of the most protected in the world. Rice was sold at a price four times higher than that at which it could be obtained from Thailand. In 1988 Japan's domestic price for wheat was eight times the world price. The situation was similar for Swiss meat and butter. The USA also spends huge amounts on farm-support programmes, though not in the same form as the EU. During 1986–90 budgetary support for farmers in the USA, the EU, and Japan accounted for some 15 per cent of government spending, comparable to what was spent on education. Not being an exporter of agricultural products, Japan, however, does not participate in the export subsidy war between the USA and the EU.

Negotiations broke down in December 1990 due to a USA–EU impasse over agriculture. Talks resumed in 1991 and by December 1993 (the very last days of the Round) a compromise was reached in which the EU agreed to a substantial reduction in export subsidies as well as a scaling down and reorientation of domestic farm-support programmes. Japan was required to admit imported rice. By 2000 she was supposed to push up imports to cover 8 per cent of domestic consumption of rice. Agriculture still remains 'special', but the Uruguay Round did succeed in putting it on a progressive liberalization track.

Major Components of the WTO Agreement on Agriculture

Domestic support

Support to producers must be reduced to 20 per cent of 1986–8 level by 1999. For developing countries the implementation period is ten years. Support is defined by a formula called Aggregate Measure of Support (AMS). For India AMS is very low and there are no reduction commitments.

Tariffs and market access

All quantitative restrictions and other NTBs are to be converted into tariffs and the level is to be gradually brought down by an average of 36 per cent over the period 1995–2000 by the DCs and by an average of 24 per cent over the period 1995–2004 by the LDCs, barring the poorest. Market access is defined to be the share of imports in domestic consumption. All countries are to provide minimum market access of 3 per cent, which is to be raised to 5 per cent within the year 2000 by the DCs and within 2004 by the LDCs.

Export competition

Export subsidies have been capped. The DCs are to reduce volume of subsidized agricultural exports by 21 per cent and spending on subsidies by 36 per cent over 1995–2000. For LDCs the figures are 14 per cent and 24 per cent over 1995–2004. Governments in LDCs, however, can continue to subsidize the cost of marketing exports of agricultural products including handling, upgrading and other processing costs, and the expenses of inland and overseas transport and freight. Export bans are precluded even in years of domestic shortage.

Big farmers in India are very excited at the prospect of emerging export opportunities. Chapter 7 treats this in more detail.

Trade in Services

Traditionally the focus in international trade has been on goods. But driven by the spectacular innovations in information and communication technology as well as government policy of deregulation and reform, trade in services has grown to outstrip the growth in merchandise trade over the last decade. Its share in world trade was almost 25 per cent in 1993, a rise of more than 5 per cent from its 1980 level. It crossed the US$ 1 trillion (thousand billion) mark in 1992. Even in the LDCs services have recorded better growth performance than other sectors of the economy. Among the DCs, for the USA competitive advantage has gradually shifted from merchandise to services such as, insurance, advertising, consultancy, communications, banking and other financial services. In 1997 earnings from services accounted for 27 per cent of total export earnings of the USA. The shift in comparative advantage prompted US policy-makers to take an active interest in the liberalization of trade in services. Lobbying by a group of financial services firms led by American Express to improve rights of establishment abroad played a key role. The developing world on the other hand, led by Argentina, Brazil, Egypt, and India, opposed the move to put services trade on the main agenda of the Uruguay Round. Its inclusion, they feared, would be used strategically by the advanced countries to marginalize the issues related to traditional commodity trade that are much more crucial for their own welfare. The fact that services include socially and politically sensitive infrastructure activity sectors is also important in explaining their reluctance. They also pointed out that the USA was trying to restrict negotiations to skill and technology intensive services requiring no relocation of buyer or seller, excluding labour intensive activities (such as construction) in which the LDCs have comparative advantage. Although the move could not be blocked, negotiations on services were put on a separate track to keep cross-issue linkages at a minimum. It was agreed that the two negotiations would be conducted within the same framework.

The Uruguay Round concluded with a two-part agreement on services. The first part, meant to lay down certain basic principles, is known as the General Agreement on Trade in Services (GATS); the second part involved specific sector-by-sector liberalization of some important types of services including telecommunications, financial services, air travel, and certain professional services. The two most prominent principles of GATS are: (i) an MFN clause, which is less general than that relating to merchandise trade because governments are given more freedom to withhold, and (ii) the principle of National Treatment, which substantially limits discrimination between foreigners and residents. Here, again, application is not automatic or universal. Every government joining GATS can submit a list of service sectors in which national treatment will apply.

Counterfeit Goods and Intellectual Property (IP)

Although trade in counterfeit goods has been around for a long time, recent advances in duplication technology have really boosted it to alarming proportions. There are bogus versions of everything in the international market. Pirated copies of books, CDs, and computer programmes are produced in abundance by countries that are lax about enforcing international copyright agreements. Some products, pharmaceuticals being a prominent example, require huge investments in R&D (Research and Development) for product or process innovations. These are typically undertaken by the MNCs in their laboratories in the advanced countries. Lax system of patent protection in many LDCs enable their sellers to be free riders and capture the domestic market through cheap imitations. Multinational business enterprises have estimated their loss in billions of dollars annually from the combined effects of outright piracy and other milder inadequacies in intellectual property protection. (Intellectual Property Rights (IPR) is commonly defined as a mix of ideas, inventions, and creative expressions that can be copyrighted or patented.) Interestingly, the finger of accusation has pointed not only to the developing countries, but to Japan as well (and to Canada occasionally). Much of Japan's spectacular technological performance can be attributed to successful imitation and adaptation of innovations developed in the western countries. The demarcation line between IPR infringement and such creative imitation (exploitation of comparative advantage in imitation and adaptation) is not easy to draw. When the DCs wanted to bring negotiations on IPR within the purview of GATT they were opposed once again by the LDCs. The latter wanted to draw a firm distinction between piracy and other IPR issues and offered to cooperate only on the former, maintaining that stronger IP protection would add to the monopoly power of MNCs and poor populations would be adversely affected through increases in the price of food and medicine. This highly contentious issue is taken up again in Chapter 7.

Trade in Clothing and Textiles

The DCs used the MFA to put very severe quantitative restrictions on imports of textiles and apparels from the LDCs. These bilaterally negotiated quotas on a country by country basis openly violated the multilateral non-discriminatory principles of GATT and inflicted heavy losses on the LDCs. Under the Agreement on Textiles and Clothing in the Uruguay Round the MFA will gradually be phased out over a ten-year period. This represents the biggest gain for the LDCs in exchange for their accession to trade-related intellectual property rights (TRIPS) and services (GATS). Chapter 7 contains more details.

PROTECTIONISM AND ITS TOOLS

The instruments which a country can use to restrict the inflow of imports are broadly classified as (a) tariffs and (b) non-tariff barriers (NTBs). Tariff is a price-related measure as it works by changing prices. NTBs apply to quantities and other attributes of traded goods and services.

Tariff

A tariff or import duty reduces the domestic demand for an imported commodity by raising its price to domestic consumers. It is also a source of revenue to the government. Tariffs are basically of two types, specific (a fixed amount per unit), or ad valorem (a specified fraction of price). The distinction is analytically unimportant, because at any moment a specific tariff has an ad valorem equivalent and vice versa. One way to calculate the average tariff rate for a country is to divide its total receipts from international trade taxes by total value of imports. It is a good proxy for the degree of protection accorded to local firms. Climbing a steady upward path India's average tariff reached an astounding peak of 53 per cent in 1987. Thereafter it has steadily come down to 24 per cent in 1998, reflecting the greater openness of the economy. By international standards the level is still fairly high. It is to be noted that the decline in tariffs has been accompanied by a rising share of foreign trade in GDP. Over the period 1988–98 the share rose almost steadily from 15.2 per cent to 24.8 per cent. (Non-tariff quantitative restrictions on India's imports were lifted fully in April 2001.)

An interesting type of policy is one where the tariff is made a function of some endogenous variable. Under a tariff quota import is free or subject to very low duty up to a certain volume and the rate of duty steps up thereafter. Variable levies are another type of policy that sets import duties to bring the foreign price up to a target level. These are used extensively by the EU to protect its agriculture.

A specific tariff, unlike an ad valorem one, changes relative prices by raising low prices proportionately more than high ones and thereby induces a substitution effect towards more expensive varieties. The average quality of imports goes up independent of any change in the preference of consumers.

To analyse the effects of a tariff the partial equilibrium demand–supply figure may be looked into once again.

The initial situation is one of free trade with world price P_w, domestic

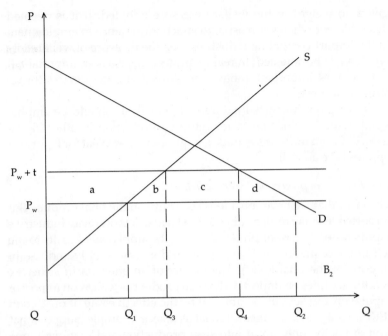

Figure 6.3: Cost of Tariff

production Q_1, demand Q_2, and import $Q_1 Q_2$. There is no difference between the domestic price of the good and its international price. If now a specific tariff of Rs t per unit is imposed, the domestic price rises to $(P_w + t)$, production expands to Q_3, demand falls to Q_4 and import, which meets the gap between demand and supply, shrinks to $Q_3 Q_4$. Consumers of the product lose on two counts: first, they pay a higher price for the amount Q_4 they continue to consume and, second, they are deprived of the benefit of consuming the units $Q_4 Q_2$ they were consuming before. Their loss in CS is the area (a + b + c + d). Domestic producers gain from the rise in price. The government obtains tariff revenue (t times the volume of import) equal to area (c). The drop in CS outweighs the sum of gains to producers and the government. This net loss from tariff is (b + d). Area (b) captures the loss to society of producing $Q_1 Q_3$ domestically at a higher cost than that of importing this amount (the production cost), area (d) represents the loss from not consuming $Q_4 Q_2$, whose marginal valuation by consumers exceeds the cost of purchasing it from the foreign source (the consumption cost).

It should be noted that the level of employment in the industry is given no weight in the welfare measure adopted. If it is deemed desirable, for whatever reason, to attach importance to employment in the import-competing industries then the measure of welfare loss will have to be adjusted. In reality, protecting jobs is an important, if not the most important, motive for tariffs and other devices for restricting imports.

Once again the partial nature of the analysis should be emphasized. Repercussions on factor returns, production in other industries, BoP, and the terms of trade are ignored. The caveat for Figure 6.1 applies here as well.

Effective rate of protection, tariff escalation

The tariff that we have considered is a duty on the final product. But imported inputs are also subjected to tariffs. A tariff on an industry's inputs raises its cost of production and its supply curve shifts to the left in consequence, implying a fall in domestic supply and rise in import (of the final good). The impact of an entire tariff structure (vector of duties on import of the final product as well as on import of inputs) on any activity is captured by the effective rate of protection (ERP). To see how it is measured let us take an example. Suppose that iron ore is the only input into steel production and that one tonne of steel (S) needs a tonne of ore (O). It is assumed that changes in tariff rates do not affect α. World prices of the two goods are P_s and P_o. At these world prices value-added V by one tonne of S production is $V = P_s - \alpha P_o$.

Let the tariff rates on imports of the goods be t_s and t_o respectively. Then at domestic prices value-added per tonne of S is $V' = P_s(1 + t_s) - \alpha P_o(1 + t_o)$.

The nominal rate of protection (NRP) is the proportionate rise in domestic price over the world price. It equals the duty on the final product.

$$NRP_s = \{P_s(1 + t_s) - P_s\}/P_s = t_s$$

The effective rate is the proportion by which value added at domestic price exceeds value added at world price as a result of the tariff structure.

$$ERP_s = (V' - V)/V = [\{P_s(1 + t_s) - \alpha P_o(1 + t_o) - (P_s - \alpha P_o)\}]/V$$

$$= \{(P_s - \alpha P_o)t_s\}/V + \{\alpha P_o(t_s - t_o)\}/V$$

$$= t_s + (\alpha P_o/V)(t_s - t_o)$$

For example, suppose that $P_s = 30$, $P_o = 20$ and $\alpha = \frac{1}{2}$. Then $V = 20$. Now tariffs of 20 per cent and 10 per cent are imposed on S and O respectively, so that $t_s = 1/5$, $t_o = 1/10$. Then ERP = 25 per cent, which is greater than the nominal tariff of 20 per cent on S.

Observations

1. If the steel industry uses no intermediate inputs ($\alpha = 0$), $ERP_s = NRP_s$.
2. If all goods (final and intermediate) are subject to a uniform rate of duty ($t_s = t_o$) then again, $ERP_s = NRP_s$.
3. If the tariff on the final good (t_s) exceeds that on the intermediate input (t_o), ERP_s will be greater than NRP_s. (Tariff structures typically cascade—duty is zero or low on raw materials, higher on intermediate goods, and highest on finished goods. Thus ERP is almost always higher than NRP.)
4. The gap between ERP and NRP varies positively with the importance of the imported input in the production of the final good, ($\alpha P_0/V$).
5. ERP may be negative if tax on the input is sufficiently larger than that on the final good. (A special case is $t_s = 0$, $t_o > 0$.) Automobile makers in countries where steel is heavily protected may find that even with a duty on automobile imports their value added is less than what it would have been under free trade. Thus, in our example, if there were no tariff on S but a 10 per cent tariff on O, then ERP = –5 per cent. The impact is a fall in value added by the steel industry.

Cascading tariff (or tariff escalation) poses problems for developing countries seeking to add value by processing raw materials. The low duty on such materials provides incentive not to process them before exporting. Import duties imposed by the DCs are much higher on processed products made from these raw materials. This bias had proved costly for countries having a comparative advantage in natural resource-based products, defined in GATT to include non-ferrous metals and minerals, forestry products, fish and fishery products. They are discouraged from moving up the value chain to progressively sophisticated processing activities. The matter was taken up in the Uruguay Round and tariff escalation was brought down along with tariff barriers.

It is very rarely the case that a country maintains a uniform tariff on the import of a particular product irrespective of the country that is exporting it. When tariff treatment depends on the country of origin the importer has to be careful in establishing a product's origin. This is far from easy in the present era of globalized production and distribution. Goods may be processed, assembled, packaged, and finished in a number of different countries or sent to the importing country via another country. A good originating in country A may pay the tariff for B where it was processed but face antidumping duties (discussed later) levied on goods from A. Regional trading arrangements which have different rates of duty for members and non-members have to be very careful in laying down and following precise rules of origin. Attempting to close off all possible loopholes, these rules often tend to become extremely cumbersome and counterproductive.

Non-tariff Barriers

The simplest NTB is a quantitative restriction on imports, known as import quota. It is usually administered by a system which prohibits imports without a licence. Up to the limit set there is no import tax, so

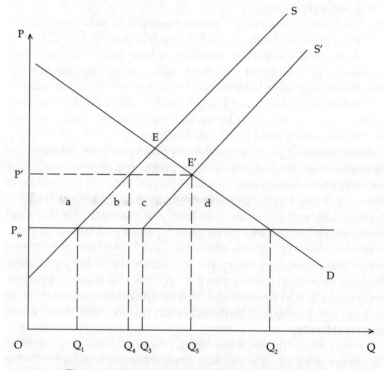

Figure 6.4: Import Quota for Competitive Industry

that the licence holders can buy at world price P_w and sell at a higher domestic price. The use of quotas is fairly extensive, applied either unilaterally or as a result of negotiated agreement between two countries.

In Figure 6.4 $Q_1 Q_2$ is the free trade level of imports for a competitive industry. If a quota of $Q_1 Q_3 < Q_1 Q_2$ is set, the domestic supply curve shifts to right by the amount of the quota and the new equilibrium is at E'. (The effect could equivalently be shown as a leftward shift of the demand curve by the amount of the quota.) The domestic price rises from P_w to P', causing domestic supply to rise to Q_4 and domestic demand to shrink to Q_5. ($Q_3 Q_1 = Q_5 Q_4$ = quota.) The change in domestic price (P' – P_w) is the tariff equivalent of the quota. One important reason why quotas are preferred over tariffs is that they are more opaque. The tariff equivalent of a quota might be several hundred per cent, a rate impossible to legislate as a tariff.

As in the case of tariff, the quota involves a loss in CS (area a + b + c + d) and a rise is PS (area a). There is no gain for the government, as it receives no revenue from imports. The area c now is the total rent or profit accruing to the holders of the quota licence who make a profit of (P' – P_w) per unit of imports. So the revenue gain of the government under the equivalent tariff exactly matches the rent of the licence holders. Counting this as part of social gain the net loss from quota is once again the area (b + d). The outcome will, however, be different if the quota gives rise to rent seeking behaviour. If real resources are expended to get hold of the import licences part or whole of the area (c) may be dissipated in rent-seeking and that part will have to be added to the social cost of quota. In the case of full dissipation the loss from quota is the area (b + c + d), making it less desirable than the equivalent tariff. Rents on import licences in Turkey have been estimated to be as high as 15 per cent of GNP in 1968 and the World Bank's 1987 World Development Report quoted estimates of 7 per cent for India and 24 per cent for Kenya.

Interestingly, the government can capture the quota rent by auctioning the licence competitively. Competition among bidders will drive the price up exactly to (P_w' – P_w) per unit of imports. In this case the welfare consequences of tariff and quota are identical. It should be stressed that the outcome depends crucially on the degree of competition in the auction. If the import good is narrowly defined and only a few bidders have information about the size of the rent involved, the market will be thin and collusion among bidders is likely to emerge to prevent the competitive outcome. Attempts to sell foreign exchange

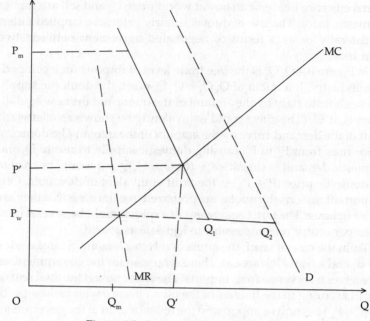

Figure 6.5: Import Quota for Monopoly

by auction in Jamaica, Zaire, Zambia, and other countries have run into this difficulty.

When the domestic market is under monopoly, a quota is preferred to a tariff by the seller. This is because a tariff acts as an effective price ceiling, whereas price setting power is preserved under a quota. Under a quota the monopolist is able to earn higher profits by reducing his quantity and charging a price higher than P_w plus the equivalent tariff. In other words, a tariff maintains competition at the margin but a quota does not. The argument is illustrated in Figure 6.5.

With an import quota of $Q_1 Q_2$ the demand curve of the domestic monopolist shifts to the left by the amount of the quota at all prices above P_w. Under competitive conditions quantity produced and sold domestically will be Q' and price will be P'. The tariff equivalent of the quota is $(P' - P_w)$. The monopoly, however, will maximize profit by producing Q_m and charging price P_m, which is higher than P'. The reduction in quantity from Q' to Q_m entails additional welfare loss. This is the reason why economists, faced with a choice between tariff and quota as instruments of protection, tend to recommend the tariff. The same principle was followed in the GATT negotiations. Countries were enjoined not to impose new quantitative restrictions and to convert existing quotas into tariffs wherever possible. Unfortunately, in the world trading economy at present quotas are very much alive and kicking in the guise of voluntary export restraints (VER).

VERs are 'orderly marketing agreements' (usually bilateral) under which exporters 'voluntarily' restrict exports of specified goods to particular markets over a given period of time. Exporters enter into such agreements because of the threat that, otherwise, even more stringent sanctions will be imposed. VERs currently cover major areas of world trade in electronics, automobiles, steel, the textiles and clothing trade between the DCs and LDCs, and numerous other items. In value terms the coverage exceeds 10 per cent of world trade. Sale of colour TV sets by Korea or Taiwan in the US market are subject to VER; Japan and the EU sign agreements each year on the number of cars to be exported to the European market. Currently over one-third of Japan's export of manufactures to other DCs is controlled by VERs.

In effect, VERs are quotas with similar welfare implications. There is one major difference. The quota rent is now captured by the exporter.

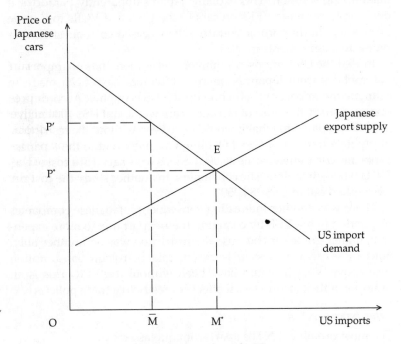

Figure 6.6: Effect of VER

Figure 6.6 illustrates the impact of a VER on Japanese export of cars. The importing country is taken to be the USA.

Under free trade, equilibrium is at E where Japanese export supply equals US import demand. The volume of imports will be M^* and price P^*. Under a VER that sets an upper limit of $\overline{M}$ on exports, E cannot be reached and price rises to P'. This rise in the price of imported cars enables the US producers to raise their price and profits. The price differential $(P' - P^*)$ per unit of imports would have been received by the US government if it had limited imports by an appropriate tariff or sold import licences through competitive auctions. But instead, it is the Japanese firms that receive it in the form of profits. The share of any individual firm in this rent will be determined by its share in $\overline{M}$, the volume of permitted exports. Allotment of VER exports among exporting firms has traditionally been done by the Ministry of International Trade and Industry (MITI) of Japan. For the group of concerned exporters VER is effectively a cartel sanctioned by the importing country. Through the enforced reduction in supply the industry is enabled to move closer to the joint profit-maximizing solution. This explains Japan's apparently paradoxical decision to continue VERs on cars to the USA and VCRs to Europe even after the importing countries had ceased to request further renewal of agreements in 1985.

In 1981 the USA imposed a limit of 1.68 million units on imports of automobiles from Japan. Numerous attempts have been made to estimate the impact of this action on the US economy. According to one such study the price of Japanese cars was about US$ 1000 higher in 1983 compared to what it would have been without the restriction, implying a transfer of US$ 1.68 billion in quota rent to the Japanese exporting companies. Some 26,000 US jobs were saved at a cost of US$ 160,000 per job to domestic consumers. In another study the cost per job worked out to US$ 284,250.

There was another interesting consequence. Japanese companies responded to the VER by changing their export mix to more expensive, higher grade cars because the restriction was on number only. Since these cars were less fuel efficient, total petroleum consumption rose above what it would have been without the VER. This is an example of the harmful social effects of restrictive trade policies.

Other types of NTBs

The most prominent NTBs apart from quotas are:

Exchange controls: These were used extensively to limit the availability of foreign exchange to traders depending on the type of transaction and the nature of the commodity traded. Requiring the permission of the Central Bank for holding a foreign currency bank account is a common method of control. Although exchange controls that impede the free flow of goods are not desirable they may be used as effective instruments to discourage speculative movements of capital in and out of a country. In the USA over the period 1963–74 exchange controls limited the ability of foreigners to borrow dollars in the country. The UK maintained strict control on borrowing until 1978.

Import deposit schemes: These rules effectively raise the cost of importing by requiring importers to deposit a sum of money, usually a proportion of the value of intended imports, with the Central Bank.

Health and safety standards: Although the ostensible purpose is to protect the welfare of domestic consumers these are often imposed to inflict high adjustment costs on foreign suppliers. Canada put restriction on import of garments from India on the ground that they did not meet Canadian standards of inflammability. The requirement insisted on by the UK government that ultra-heat-treated milk should be 'filled and closed on registered premises' effectively prevented the sale of foreign milk because only local authorities could register such premises. A more recent case concerns the import of meat into the EU from the USA and Canada. The Union alleged that the animals had been treated with certain hormones (not used in Europe) that are harmful for human beings. The US regarded the claim as an example of pure protectionism. There was virtually no meat export from the USA to the EU in 1989–90. Advanced industrial countries, fearful of competition from low-wage developing countries, have started demanding compliance with core labour standards and environmental standards by their trading partners. The LDCs rightly look upon this as protectionism in disguise. The issue is taken up again in Chapter 7.

Customs valuation procedure: This is a major NTB. The duty under ad valorem tariff can be raised by artificially inflating the value of imports. The most notorious post-war example was the US practice of valuing certain chemical imports not at their invoice price or any other 'world price', but at 'American selling price'. This procedure was abolished after the Tokyo Round. Imposition of time consuming formalities (bureaucratic delays) are also used as effective barriers to trade. The French decision in 1982 to require all VCR imports to pass through the small inland customs station of Poitiers (manned by a staff of just eight) is a famous example.

Government procurements or public sector contracts have always been an important field of discrimination between domestic and foreign suppliers. Tenders for public projects are usually not internationally publicized and in many countries explicit margins of preference exist for domestic firms. The Tokyo Round sought to work out an international code to regulate the use of government procurement as an NTB.

A study carried out by the Organization for Economic Cooperation and Development (OECD) in 1992 made an attempt to quantify the global cost of protection. Two scenarios were considered: (a) a 30 per cent reduction in tariffs (roughly equivalent to that achieved in the Tokyo and Uruguay Rounds) and (b) complete elimination of tariffs. World output was estimated to rise by US$ 195 billion per annum within a decade under (a) and by US$ 477 billion per annum within a decade under (b). The anticipated loss (to mainly net importers of food) could be fully compensated by a transfer of resources amounting to only 3.5 per cent of the anticipated gains.

The Case for Protection

In some cases use of tariffs and NTBs on selective basis can be justified. They are: (a) to prevent dumping, (b) to protect infant industries, and (c) to induce foreign investment in the domestic economy.

Dumping occurs when a good is sold in an overseas market at less than the home price or less than its average total cost of production including overheads (fixed costs). A modified method that is widely used allows a 'reasonable margin of profit' to be added to average cost to arrive at a 'fair price'. Dumping occurs when the actual price is smaller than this fair or normal price.

A prohibition against dumping was included in GATT (Article 6), because dumping is considered a predatory practice. By temporarily suffering losses a strong firm may succeed in driving out weaker rivals and reap high monopoly profits thereafter. Consumers enjoy low prices in the initial phase but suffer ultimately when the successful predator begins to exploit its market power. By the end of the 1990s most trading nations had adopted antidumping laws. More than one thousand actions were initiated between July 1980 and June

1988. The proceedings are typically set in motion by complaints from domestic producers. The foreign supplier is requested to submit home market price and cost information so that the fair price may be calculated. It should come as no surprise that the procedure is blatantly biased in favour of a positive finding. US investigators, for example, often used an 8 per cent return on capital to construct the fair price, although the return was much lower in the domestic industries seeking antidumping action. The high frequency of complaints by inefficient firms shows that the rule against dumping has become a very popular way for such firms to obtain protection against imports.

From the economists' point of view the flaw in the standard tests for dumping can be illustrated by cases where a firm may violate them without any predatory intent. The first case comes straight out of elementary microeconomics. A profit maximizing monopolist who sells his product in two separate markets, domestic and foreign, will charge a lower price in the foreign market if the price elasticity of demand is higher there (possibly due to the presence of more substitutes). This price differential has nothing to do with predation. The cost of production test is defective because there are circumstances, a recession in the industry depressing demand temporarily, for example, when it is rational policy on the part of the firm to continue operation even if price fails to cover its full average costs (see the section on predatory pricing in Chapter 3). Now this is a question of survival, not predation!

In view of these defects attempts were made in the Uruguay Round to reform and harmonize the existing antidumping laws. The new WTO Antidumping Agreement aims at reducing the protectionist bias of the investigating methods of the past and a new clause has been added—antidumping duties are to be terminated within five years of imposition, unless a review decides that their removal would be likely to lead to a recurrence of dumping and injury to domestic producers. Also, duties may not be imposed if dumping margins are less than 2 per cent. Apart from this no major change could be effected, owing chiefly to the opposition by the USA and Canada, the two biggest users of antidumping laws.

Changes in the existing antidumping rules required implementing legislation in the USA. Inevitably, this provoked opposition by domestic lobbies. The Clinton Administration responded to the pressure by proposing other amendments in the law—amendments permitted but not required by the Agreement—that were actually more restrictive than the existing laws! Such strange outcomes are possible because WTO agreements do not have any direct effect on the domestic legal order.

The 1988 protocol between Australia and New Zealand, pursuant to the Australia–New Zealand Closer Economic Relations Trade Agreement (ANZCERTA) was a much more positive step in this respect. There was agreement that as of July 1990 all antidumping actions between the two countries would cease and any antidumping duty then in place would be terminated. Harmonized provisions in the competition laws of both countries were substituted.

The original GATT also contained a prohibition against export subsidies, because they give a competitive advantage to exporters that is not derived from efficiency. An importing country was permitted to impose countervailing duties on imports that have received subsidies from their home governments. In recent years the usage has been growing rapidly; for example, about 40 per cent of US imports from India have been subjected to countervailing duties. The USA has been the largest user of these duties, initiating over one hundred investigations since 1985. What actually constitutes a subsidy is not always easy to decide, because many countries subsidize their exports indirectly. Measures include low interest on export credit, preferential tax treatment of export profits, wage subsidies, and various investment incentives. Are countervailing duties justified even if there is no direct export subsidy? Furthermore, subsidies are widely used to achieve domestic goals such as aiding depressed regions, encouraging modernization of declining industries and so on. If some industry receives the benefit of a subsidy because it is located in a depressed region, should its export be penalized? These are thorny issues that generate much international friction. The Tokyo Round broadened the earlier prohibition of export subsidies and allowed governments to impose countervailing duties even though subsidies were not directly on exports. An exception was allowed for developing countries, who could subsidize manufactured exports but had to reduce the subsidies once they became 'inconsistent with competitive development needs'. Arguing that they have outgrown the need to subsidize their exports, the USA began to slap countervailing duties on imports from Argentina, Brazil, and other LDCs.

During the Uruguay Round the GATT code relating to subsidies was amended. A distinction was made between different types of subsidies depending on their impact on trade and their objectives. A 'Green Box' contains subsidies that have a broad developmental impact (education, general infrastructure, basic R&D) or have non economic rationale (regional imbalance, income support). Subsidies that are not in this box can be countervailed, but at least a quarter of the firms in a domestic industry must support the launching of a duty investigation. A duty can continue after five years only if, as in the case of dumping, a review committee can definitely demonstrate that abolition will lead to the recurrence or continuation of material injury to domestic suppliers. Relatively advanced developing countries are given an eight-year period to abolish their export subsidies. The EU had to agree to a drastic reform of its policy of subsidizing the export of surplus farm products.

Infant industry protection

The use of protection to establish and nurture new industries is widely supported. The textiles industry in the UK that played a key role in the Industrial Revolution in the eighteenth century would not have survived without protection from Asian competition. Economic development in the USA, Canada, France, and Germany took place behind high tariff walls. Japan's rise as an industrial power owes a lot to the government's successful policy of picking winners and assisting their growth with appropriate modes of protection. Article 18 of GATT permitted the developing countries to use trade barriers for protecting infant industries from foreign competition during the initial period. It was hoped that it would enable them to acquire competitive muscle by absorbing the benefits of both economy of scale and economy of experience or learning by doing (see Glossary). The EU used the infant industry logic to justify protection of its emerging high technology industries. In some cases it was successful.

The fundamental problem with the otherwise unassailable infant industry logic is that policy-makers in LDCs have shown great vulnerability to capture by rent seeking special interests in the initial decision to promote and subsequent decisions to indefinitely support an infant industry. This may be termed the perpetual infancy syndrome. Examples can be given by the dozen from Asia, Africa, and Latin America.

Strategic protection and DFI

Trade protection can be, and has been, used as a strategy to entice inward foreign investment. In fact, gaining access to host country markets sheltered behind high tariff walls has been one of the major driving forces of DFI in the post-war years. Relocation of production brings local firms into contact with advanced techniques and managerial methods and, most importantly, creates more jobs. The consumers will still be worse off than under liberalized trade because the domestically producing foreign firm will be able to price right up to the tariff. Effective price control and other regulation may check this without killing off the attractions of relocation.

A disturbing possibility is that protection may have to continue indefinitely. If comparative advantage has genuinely been transferred to the host country, it may be profitable to continue operation even after the removal of protection. But the large scale closure of American firms in Canada and their movement back to the USA in the wake of the Canada–US Free Trade Agreement is a reminder that the strategic use of protection may not be an efficient policy from the long term capability building point of view. It is important to attach conditions that actually facilitate a real transfer of comparative advantage such as requirements for reinvestment and training of workers. Enforcing such requirements, however, may be beyond the administrative capability of governments in most LDCs. It is difficult even in a developed country, as is amply demonstrated in the Canadian case.

REGIONAL TRADING BLOCS

Along with the evolution of the multilateral trading system under the guidance of the GATT there has also been a parallel movement towards the formation of RTBs. Although they constitute a violation of the MFN principle of non-discrimination embodied in the GATT, their formation was permitted because they were viewed as building blocks for a world order in which universal free trade will ultimately prevail. But the upsurge of new protectionism in the DCs in recent years (especially quantitative restrictions and other NTBs) giving rise to acute trade friction between the USA, the EU, and Japan has caused many analysts to take a more gloomy view of the future. RTBs, they fear, will be looking inwards more and more and begin to behave as regional fortresses. A regime of entrenched regionalism, rather than universal free trade, will take over.

In fact, intraregional trading has assumed such importance that some analysts are asserting that globalization (in the sense of production and distribution of goods and services of a homogeneous type and quality on a worldwide basis) is a myth. In support of their claim they cite the following facts:

More than 85 per cent of all automobiles produced in North America

---

BOX 6.2: RTBs and their Members

ACM (Arab Common Market): Egypt, Iraq, Jordan, Libya, Syria, and Yemen

AFTA (Asian Free Trade Area): Brunei, Indonesia, Malaysia, Philippines, and Singapore

ANCOM (Andean Common Market): Bolivia, Colombia, Ecuador, Peru, and Venezuela

APEC (Asia Pacific Economic Cooperation Forum): AFTA and NAFTA members plus Australia, China, Hong Kong, Japan, Korea, New Zealand, New Guinea, and Taiwan

ASEAN (Association of South East Asian Nations): Brunei, Indonesia, Malaysia, Philippines, Singapore, and Thailand

CARICOM (Caribbean Community): Belize plus most English speaking island states in the Caribbean

CEFTA (Central European Free Trade Area): Czech and Slovak Republics, Hungary, and Poland

EFTA (European Free Trade Association): Iceland, Liechtenstein, Norway, and Switzerland

EU (European Union): Austria, Belgium, Denmark, Finland, France, Germany, Greece, Ireland, Italy, Luxembourg, Holland, Portugal, Spain, Sweden, and the UK

GCC (Gulf Cooperation Council): Bahrain, Kuwait, Oman, Qatar, Saudi Arabia, and UAE

MERCOSUR (Southern Cone Common Market): Argentina, Brazil, Paraguay, and Uruguay

NAFTA (North American Free Trade Agreement): Canada, Mexico, and the USA

---

are built in North American factories, over 90 per cent of cars produced in the EU are sold there, more than 93 per cent of all cars registered in Japan are made in Japan. In services, employing about 70 per cent of the workforce in North America, Western Europe, and Japan, activities are essentially local and regional.

Intraregional trade accounts for a significant proportion of the total trade of the broad triad consisting of the EU, NAFTA, and Japan–Asia (comprising Japan, Australia, New Zealand, China, Taiwan, Hong Kong, India, Indonesia, Malaysia, Philippines, Singapore, and Thailand). For the year 1997 the percentage share of intrabloc trade in total trade was 60.6 for the EU, 49.1 for NAFTA, and 53.1 for Asia. Whether these figures are high enough to render globalization a myth remains a moot point, but their magnitude cannot be denied.

RTBs are usually classified into four types:

1) Free Trade Areas (FTA): Member countries reduce or abolish trade barriers among themselves while maintaining individual barriers against non-members.

2) Customs Union (CU): In addition to eliminating trade barriers among themselves a common external tariff is imposed by the members on import from outside countries.

3) Common Market: The CU is extended to movements of factors of production as well.

4) Economic Union: There is a single currency and national economic policies are coordinated and harmonized within a common market.

Article 24 of GATT allowed the creation of FTAs and CUs subject to the following conditions: (i) trade barriers after integration do not rise on average; (ii) trade restrictions on 'substantially all' intraregional exchanges of goods are eliminated within a 'reasonable' length of time, and (iii) the proposal is notified to GATT, which may establish a Working Party to check if these conditions are satisfied.

The language of the article is ambiguous and open to interpretations. There never was any serious attempt to apply the tests, however, mostly for political reasons. Under covert threat by the six original members to withdraw from GATT, the formation of the EEC was passed without close scrutiny and this created a precedent that was subsequently followed. The Uruguay Round also was content to reaffirm that RTBs should 'to the greatest possible extent avoid creating adverse effects on the trade of other members'. Disciplines are still lacking with respect to preferential rules of origin and there is no requirement that RTBs be open to new members who are willing to satisfy their obligations. The surveillance mechanism is no stronger than before, the WTO having no mandate to monitor the trade effects of RTBs.

The Welfare Effect of Trading Blocs

There has been much debate as to whether the formation of RTBs is beneficial or not. From a member country's point of view the net impact depends on the balance between two opposite effects: trade creation and trade diversion. Consider an initial situation where country A, country B, and the rest of the world R trade with each other under tariffs. A and B then form a CU and abolish all tariffs on each other's imports, but maintain a common tariff on R. There is no change in R's trade policy. The elimination of tariffs between A and B is a move to free trade and each can now concentrate more on the goods in which it has a comparative advantage relative to the other. Trade expands and both enjoy more gains. This is the positive trade creation effect. The negative effect of trade diversion may be illustrated with a simple example. Suppose that before the formation of the CU the price of a particular commodity X was 10 in B and 8 in R and that A had a specific tariff of 5 on X. A was importing X from R, the cheaper source (tariff-inclusive prices were 15 and 13 for B and R respectively). After the abolition of tariff on B, but not on R, consumers of A buy X from B which is now the cheaper source. This diversion or switch is harmful because the cheaper outside source has been priced out by discriminatory tariff. If, before integration, most of A's trade is with B, trade creation will dominate trade diversion and the RTB will be beneficial. Also the magnitude of the trade diversion will depend positively on the gap between B's price and the price of R. Figure 6.7 explains the situation.

The price of B's good P_B lies between the rest of the world's price P_R and the tariff inclusive price in A, $P_A (= P_R+t)$. A is importing $Q_2 Q_3$ from R. After the withdrawal of tariff on B, there is a switch from R to

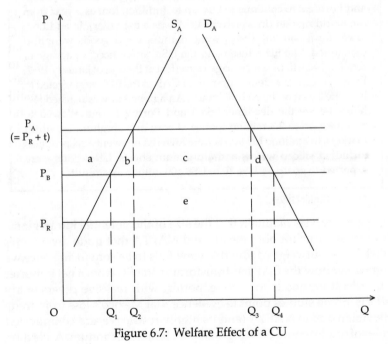

Figure 6.7: Welfare Effect of a CU

B as the source of imports. The domestic price of A falls to P_B and imports rise to $Q_1 Q_4$. The impact is: (a) B's goods displace domestic production, $Q_1 Q_2$, (b) Lower price stimulates consumption, $Q_3 Q_4$, and (c) B's goods displace imports from R, $Q_2 Q_3$. The gain in CS and the loss in PS are the familiar areas (a + b + c + d) and the foregone tariff revenue is (c + e). The net welfare gain is (b + d – e), which may be positive or negative. The closer P_B is to P_R the less likely is the arrangement to be harmful.

Country R is hurt by the union because it has lost its export market in A. Countries in such a situation are entitled under the GATT to compensation in the form of concessions that would enable them to increase exports of some other goods. This has the potential to become explosive. Box 6.3 contains a case study.

BOX 6.3: Effect on Non-member

When Spain and Portugal came under the CAP after joining the EU in 1986, the USA was threatened with the loss of 2.8 million tonnes of corn and sorghum exports to Spain, worth approximately US$ 430 million a year. In compensation it demanded that the EU allow Spain and Portugal to continue to buy up to 4 million tonnes a year from the world market (in which the USA was a big seller). In addition, lower tariffs on imports of some manufactured goods were also demanded. The EU refused and the USA announced a package of retaliatory tariff measures to go into effect at the end of January 1987. France, the most ardent supporter of CAP in the EU, was targeted to bear the brunt of the counterattack. An agreement was reached just hours before the deadline. Spain and Portugal were allowed to purchase up to 2.3 million tonnes of corn and sorghum on world markets. In addition EU tariffs were lowered on twenty-six products including silicon wafers and aluminium sheets. US exports were expected to go up by US$ 70 to US$ 100 million as a result.

Source: Ethier (1995).

Some analysts maintain that the size of the potential intraregional trade is so large for both the EU and NAFTA that trade diversion is likely to be outweighed. But this view fails to be convincing once we remember how the CAP has transformed the EU from a net importer of agriculture goods to a net exporter, with massive diversionary effects. Some studies point to evidence that Mexico's loss from trade diversion due to NAFTA (and its highly restrictive and complicated rules of origin) could be as high as US$ 3 billion per annum. According to World Bank estimates, approximately 36 per cent of Caribbean exports to the USA will be displaced. These figures have been challenged by the supporters of regional integration. Empirical evidence is inconclusive and economists remain deeply divided on the issue.

THE EUROPEAN UNION

The EU is by far the most successful RTB in history. It is more than a CU, something between a common market and an economic union. Actually, an economic and political unification of Europe is the ultimate goal. (The customs union, Zollverein, in the past had played an important role in the unification of petty German states under Prussian dominance.) The first step was the signing of the European Coal and Steel Community Treaty in 1951 under which France, Germany, Italy, and the three BENELUX (Belgium, Netherlands, and Luxembourg) countries accepted a supranational authority over the two industries to regulate pricing policies and commercial practices.

The Treaty of Rome of 1957, signed by the same six countries, established the EEC. Several institutions were created for the realization of the treaty norms: the European Court of Justice, the European Commission, the Council of Ministers, and the European Parliament. The Council, consisting of political representatives from member states, makes regulation and directives upon the initiative of the Commission. Some of the most important provisions are directly enforceable by the European Court. The court takes cases from individual citizens, as well as from governments and institutions. The European Parliament is elected directly by voters in the member countries.

Seven other European countries, opposed to some major provisions of the Rome Treaty, created the European Free Trade Association (EFTA) in 1959. (Austria, Finland, Sweden, and the UK left later, not all at the same time, to join the EEC.) In 1961 the UK, Denmark, and Norway applied for membership. Britain's application was vetoed by France in 1963. A second application was accepted in 1973 and the UK, Denmark, and Ireland became members. Norway had withdrawn her application following a negative verdict in a domestic referendum. There are fifteen members at present and many more countries, mostly of the former communist bloc, are waiting to join.

During the 1960s the EEC successfully carried out dismantling of tariffs on intraregional trade and participated vigorously in the Kennedy Round of GATT negotiations. The CAP was adopted in

1968, and the EMS in 1979. A currency composite ecu was created, something like the Special Drawing Right (SDR) of the IMF to be used for official transactions within the Union. Soon the ecu was embraced even by the private sector which began to denominate bond issues and other financial transactions in ecus. But the most significant success was in the area of exchange rate management. A system of adjustable pegs was established for the exchange rates of the member currencies relative to each other. The central banks undertook to maintain market rates within 2.25 per cent of these pegs. This was the European Exchange Rate Mechanism (ERM). For many years the EMS functioned admirably well.

By the 1980s, however, there was already a growing feeling that the force of integration was slackening and the Union was in danger of becoming a clumsy machinery for administering a monstrously wasteful and inequitable farm-support programme. In 1985 the European Commission issued a white paper calling for the 'completion of the internal market' by 1 January 1993. The deadline gave the programme its name, 'Europe 1992' or simply '1992'. The Single European Act was approved in 1986, allowing many important decisions to be made by weighted majority voting instead of requiring unanimity by giving each member a veto. To get around the thorny problem of harmonization of regulatory policies the members agreed to the mutual recognition of regulations. A product approved for sale in, say, France can be sold freely in any other member country. The white paper also contained hundreds of proposals for harmonization of policies with respect to financial services, company law, insurance, securities, and telecommunications. The target was to achieve, by the end of 1992, a Europe without frontiers in which residents would possess the four freedoms—to trade, to migrate, to invest, and to conduct business irrespective of national borders. Many people were sceptical that '1992' would not amount to much, but they were proved wrong. The programme was basically successful. Border checks have not entirely disappeared and many NTBs are still administered at the national level, but remarkable progress has undoubtedly been achieved.

In 1991 the members agreed to a major revision of the original Treaty of Rome. The new agreement, known as the Maastricht Treaty, is intended to be a blueprint for a fundamental deepening of European integration. The most radical and ambitious aspect was the plan for the creation of a single European currency (the euro) by the end of the twentieth century as a crucial step toward a full-fledged monetary union. In 1999 eleven countries accepted the euro as their common currency and established a new institution, the European Central Bank to conduct monetary policy. The programme, however, has also run into some formidable economic and political difficulties. Several countries have retained the option not to participate in various parts of the agreement. The UK, for example, has declined to participate in the harmonization of social policy. Provisions relating to immigration policy have provoked strong reaction by the right and extreme right in a number of countries where immigration is a highly sensitive political issue. Most serious perhaps was the virtual collapse in 1992–3 of the existing arrangements for coordination of exchange rates. Italy and the UK left the EMS and the ability of the EU to sustain monetary integration around a single currency has been thrown into considerable doubt. Widespread scepticism persists, but the EU keeps lumbering along towards its goal of the United States of Europe.

SEVEN

Developing Countries in the New International Economic Order

The GATT was meant to be a purely interim arrangement, a framework for initiating the process of multilateral trade liberalization until the establishment of the International Trade Organization (ITO). But since the ITO never came into being, the GATT had to assume the responsibilities of a supranational organization. It was, however, increasingly felt during the 1980s that in the context of major changes in the world economy the GATT was due for a thorough review and reform.

The forces that had a radical impact on the world trading system and put severe strain on the administrative capabilities of the GATT were broadly: (a) the acceleration of globalized manufacturing brought about by ever-rising DFI by MNCs and the emergence of the East Asian NICs as global players; (b) the evolution of the EU and formation of NAFTA and other organizations for preferential regional trading; and (c) the collapse of the centrally planned economies and their subsequent efforts to develop market economies. A large number of LDCs in Asia, Africa, and Latin America decided to move away from import substitution under extensive state control towards a much more liberal policy stance. They wanted to participate fully in the global trading system by opening up their economies to foreign trade and investment.

THE WORLD TRADE ORGANIZATION

The proposal to establish a Multilateral Trade Organisation came from Canada in 1990, supported by the EU. The idea was to convert

the GATT from a trade agreement into a full-fledged membership
organization to tie together in a unified institutional framework the
modified GATT, the GATS, and all other agreements concluded
under the auspices of the Uruguay Round and its predecessors. After
some modification, including a change of name, the proposal was
accepted and the Final Act establishing the WTO was signed in
Marrakesh on 15 April 1994. Each country joining the WTO is bound
by all the agreements. In this sense the Uruguay Round substituted a
single undertaking for the separate and disparate obligations assumed by various governments in the earlier rounds. In cooperation
with the other two Bretton Woods institutions, the IMF and the
World Bank, the new institution is expected to achieve 'greater co-
herence in global economic policy making' (Article 3, WTO). Unlike

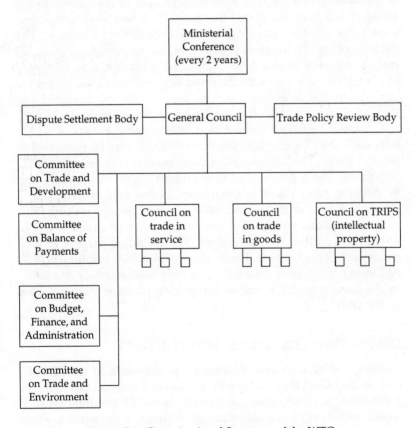

Figure 7.1: Organizational Structure of the WTO

the IMF and the World Bank where voting rights are determined by the financial stakes of governments, the WTO is governed by the system of 'one nation one vote'.

Figure 7.1 presents the organizational structure of the WTO.

The WTO has introduced major changes in the dispute settlement mechanism to make it less time consuming and more automatic and binding than it had been under GATT 1947. In the pre-Uruguay days when any government brought a charge of non-compliance or violation of obligation against any other, a panel of experts was appointed to investigate and make recommendations. But the defendant's consent to the appointment of the panel was required and the defendant had the power to veto the verdict too. There was also no time limit on the process. Dissatisfaction had been growing steadily through the years and reached its peak with an explosion of complaints in the 1980s. (It has been calculated that more than half of all complaints were lodged in the last of the four decades of GATT history.) The decision of the US Congress to adopt Section 301, which gives the US president power to take drastic unilateral measures, was prompted by acute dissatisfaction with the prevailing arrangements. Under the new system the defendant's powers are considerably curtailed and the complainant is entitled to settlement within a reasonable period.

If informal bilateral consultation fails to settle a dispute within sixty days the Dispute Settlement Body (DSB) may be requested to set up a panel. The background documentation is done by the WTO secretariat. The panel must submit a report within nine months and its decision takes effect automatically. In the case of an appeal a standing Appellate Body, composed of seven persons serving four-year terms, deals with it. The Body must make its decision within sixty days and this decision is final. The offending party is given a reasonable period of time if immediate compliance is impracticable. At the end of this period it must pay compensation or face retaliation by the complainant. The authorization for retaliation will be granted by the DSB.

DEVELOPING COUNTRIES AND THE GATT

Although some developing countries participated in GATT 1947, and ten acceeded, they had hardly any say in the negotiations. By the 1960s the LDCs had numerical majority in GATT and their share in world trade had grown substantially. (Currently the share is about 25 per cent in both world exports and imports.) The frustrations at being marginalized led to attempts to evolve other fora where they could exert more influence. Under the stewardship of Raul Prebisch, an Argentinian economist, the United Nations Conference on Trade and Development (UNCTAD) was created in 1964 for this purpose. A political bloc of developing countries in the UN, called the 'Group of 77', was also formed in the same year.

Article 18 of GATT recognized the need for development-based exceptions from GATT strictures. In 1954–5 it was modified to allow quantitative restrictions to be used for BoP purposes whenever foreign exchange reserves fell below what was considered necessary for economic development. The infant industry view for protection was accepted and incorporated, as revealed in the statement:

(developing countries) should enjoy additional facilities to enable them (a) to maintain sufficient flexibility in their tariff structure to be able to grant the tariff protection required for the establishment of a particular industry and (b) to apply quantitative restrictions for balance of payments purpose which take full account of the continued high level of demand for imports likely to be generated by their programme of economic development. (Article 18.2)

In response to insistent demands voiced through UNCTAD a new Part IV, entitled 'Trade and Development', was added in 1965. The DCs were exhorted to give effect to commitments to reduce or eliminate trade barriers against exports from the LDCs. Unlike other provisions of the General Agreement, Part IV, however, did not carry binding obligations.

UNCTAD initiated the 'Generalized System of Preference' (GSP) in 1968 with the intent of extending the existing system of colonial preference under which the ex-colonial powers accorded favourable treatment to the exports and imports of their ex-colonies. The USA and other DCs accepted GSP and agreed to grant tariff preferences to LDCs on a non-reciprocal basis. The preferences, however, were not 'bound' and, therefore, could be removed or modified at any time. More importantly, GSP excludes product groups that are of significant interest to LDCs, such as steel, textiles, clothing, and footwear. It also does not adequately address the problem of 'tariff escalation' which makes it harder for the developing countries to move up the value chain. Upper limits on the quantities that were to be imported at preferential rates were set on the ground that any country capable of supplying large amounts did not really require the assistance of lower trade barriers. Any positive effect the GSP had on investment plans to expand exports to exploit preferential rates, was seriously dampened thereby. The decision of the USA to graduate Hong Kong, Singapore, South Korea, and Taiwan from its GSP scheme in 1989 had a similar effect on the respective economies. Careful empirical research has concluded that exports from LDCs are higher than they would have been without the GSP, but the incremental amounts are rather small.

The Lome Convention is another mechanism for granting non-reciprocal trade preferences to the LDCs. It first came into force in 1975 and has been renewed several times since then. In addition to trade preference the Convention contains a wide ranging agenda for commercial cooperation between the EU and some sixty-five ex-colonies.

In the Tokyo Round, in which more than seventy LDCs participated, the developing countries were exempted from the general ban on export subsidies, provided that these subsidies are not 'used in a manner which causes serious prejudice to the trade or production of another signatory'. The Enabling Clause was adopted which introduced the concept of 'special and differential treatment' and created a permanent legal basis for the operation of GSP. The quid pro quo was the inclusion of a graduation principle, but the actual criterion for graduation was not clearly set out. According to the US Trade Act of 1974, amended in 1984, graduation from GSP status takes place once an LDC crosses the level of US$ 8500 GDP per capita. Some of the more affluent NICs are now beginning to cross this relatively high threshold. (The Act also gives the US president authority to waive GSP status if the country fails to provide reasonable access to its markets and adequate protection of IPR.)

The Multifibre Arrangement

The MFA is a framework for VERs, limiting the exports of textiles and clothing from thirty-one developing 'low wage' countries to nine developed ones. Next to agriculture, textiles and clothing formed the second major sector that was not covered by GATT 1947 disciplines. Currently these products account for no less than 7–8 per cent of world trade. Being labour intensive and relatively low technology activities they also constitute the most important avenue of access to prosperity for the developing countries. Protectionism in the DCs was driven by the desire to maintain jobs for unskilled or semiskilled workers. Box 7.1 contains a history of the managed trade in textiles and clothing.

It should be noted that despite the existence of a monitoring agent,

---

BOX 7.1: A Chronology of Managed Trade in Textiles

1955:   'voluntary' export restraints on cotton textiles intro-
            duced by Japan at the request of the USA
1956:   VER extended by Japan
1959–60:   Hong Kong, India, and Pakistan impose VER on cotton
            textiles export to the UK
1960:   The Short Term Arrangement on cotton textiles is nego-
            tiated in July
1962:   The Long term Agreement Regarding International
            Trade in Cotton Textiles (LTA) imposes a 5 per cent
            growth limit on imports of cotton products and puts an
            important part of the North–South trade in textiles
            under a managed trade regime
1967:   LTA is extended for the next three years
1970:   LTA is extended for another three years
1973:   The USA persuades major LDC garment exporters to
            accept a Multifibre Arrangement(MFA). Without this
            the domestic textiles lobby would have blocked the
            USA's participation in the Tokyo Round. Permitted
            import growth is more liberal than under the LTA
1974:   MFA limits the growth of textiles and clothing imports
            to 6 per cent per annum. A Textiles Surveillance Body
            supervises the implementation of the MFA under the
            auspices of the GATT Textiles Committee. The Com-
            mittee is composed of the parties to the Arrangement
1977:   Extension agreed for a five-year period (MFA–II)
1982:   MFA–III is negotiated, extending the Arrangement for
            five more years
1985:   Developing countries covered by the MFA establish an
            International Textile and Clothing Bureau to speed up
            elimination of the Arrangement and the return of tex-
            tiles and clothing trade to GATT
1986:   MFA is extended up to 1991 (MFA–IV)
1991:   MFA is extended up to 1994

Source: Adapted from Pomfret (1991).

the Textile Surveillance Body, importing countries have often taken
additional restrictive measures beyond the Arrangement.

There is a consensus that the LDCs have suffered huge losses
because of the MFA. An UNCTAD study in 1986 concluded that

complete elimination of trade barriers would boost total export of clothing by 135 per cent while textile export would grow by 80 per cent. More recent studies put the potential gains at even higher levels. Table 7.1 gives the estimated rise in trade in clothing for selected Asian countries following the liberalization of MFA.

Table 7.1: Projected Increase in Clothing Trade after MFA Phaseout (per cent of total bilateral trade)

Trading partner	Bangladesh	India	Nepal	Sri Lanka	Pakistan
USA	12.9	2.6	8.4	9.0	3.5
EU	9.8	4.3	10.0	3.8	6.4
Japan	0.1	0.2	0.1	0.1	0.1

Source: Srinivasan (1998)

The Uruguay Round contained a plan for a sweeping reform and eventual phasing out of the MFA. Trade in clothing and textiles will be integrated into GATT rules and liberalized over a ten-year period. The proposed integration, however, is heavily backloaded, putting off most of the liberalization for the future. Under the Agreement on Textile and Clothing all MFA-based or bilaterally-agreed quantitative restrictions are to be removed on products accounting for at least 16 per cent of total value of imports of the members in 1990. Within three years members must remove remaining restrictions on products accounting for a further 17 per cent of total imports. Removal on at least another 18 per cent is required after seven years. All remaining restrictions must go by 2004. Thus the extent of backloading is as high as 49 per cent of the value of 1990-imports. During the adjustment period quotas are to be expanded substantially to accustom the import competing industries to the rigours of competition. A 6 per cent permitted growth rate of quotas in 1994 will become 7 per cent per year in 1995–7, 8.7 per cent during 1998–2001, and 11 per cent during 2002–4.

The phasing out of the MFA is a major achievement for the LDCs who insisted on it as a quid pro quo for the agreement on TRIPS and services. It has, however, to be emphasized that liberalization commitments will not deprive the DCs of their power to levy tariffs. Although the average tariff will come down as a result of the Uruguay Round, import duties on many textiles and clothing items (and footwear) will remain in place at levels much higher than the average for manufactured products in general. Domestic producers of the importing countries will also definitely pressurize their governments into using antidumping actions with greater frequency in the future.

The distribution of gains from the abolition of MFA will be determined by the relative efficiencies of the exporting LDCs. The quotas currently protect some inefficient producers who may be driven out in a more competitive regime. India's position is not very secure in this respect. Some DCs such as Italy have benefited from the MFA restrictions on Asian competitors to become major clothing exporters in the 1980s. Actually, during recent years, most of our MFA quotas have remained underutilized, presumably owing to high costs of production. Without considerable upgradation of technology, quality, and marketing capability Indian firms will find it very hard to maintain, let alone increase, their share in the expanding, and more liberalized, global market.

TRADE AND LABOUR RIGHTS

Recurring international debates and discussions relating to workers' rights led to the creation of the International Labour Organization (ILO) in 1919. In consultation with employers, trade unions, and governments the ILO, as of 1994, had passed over 180 conventions dealing with various aspects of working conditions. But these are not binding and most countries have accepted only a small number. (The USA has, to date, ratified less than two dozen.)

In the current context of liberalization and global integration governments of many advanced countries, under intense pressure from producers' lobbies, have begun to draw a distinction between free trade and 'fair trade' and argue that it is unfair to expose their producers to competition from countries with low wage rates and poor labour standards. A related complaint is the familiar 'race to the bottom' argument, according to which workers in the advanced industrial countries will have to lower their own standards to remain competitive. Otherwise, it is feared, footloose capital will depart for the lower cost LDCs.

The USA and France took the initiative in inserting the labour standard issue in the final stage of the Uruguay Round. The objective was to introduce a Social Clause specifying minimum standards in this area. Non-compliance will be treated as 'social dumping' and will attract antidumping duties. The 'core' labour rights include: the

---

BOX 7.2: Core Conventions of the ILO

Out of over 180 existing conventions the ILO has identified seven 'core conventions' as fundamental. These conventions are relevant to all employers, including MNCs and their affiliates. They include:

- Two conventions concerning the abolition of forced labour. These are the least contentious and most widely adopted.
- Two conventions assuring basic rights for both employers and workers: freedom of association and the right to organize and the right to collective bargaining.
- Two conventions regarding discrimination: one prohibiting discrimination on the basis of race, colour, sex, religion, political opinion, national extraction, or social origin and the other on equal remuneration for men and women workers for work of equal value.
- The minimum age convention which stipulates that adolescents cannot be employed before the end of compulsory schooling and at least fourteen years of age.
- The convention on minimum wage fixing.
- The convention on the working environment (air pollution, noise, and vibration).
- The convention on home workers from whom many MNCs in developing countries source most of, or even all, their supply of products such as garments, footwear, or toys.

The Tripartite Declaration of Principles concerning Multinational Enterprises and Social Policy exhorts governments to ratify core conventions and MNCs to comply with them. Governments, multinationals, and trade unions report to the Governing Body of the ILO every three years on the effect given to the Declaration.

Source: ILO Reports.

right to collective bargaining and freedom of association, the right not to be enslaved, the abolition of child labour, and equality of opportunity of employment for men and women. The USA and other OECD countries wanted to make compliance with core standards a precondition for access to their markets.

The LDCs countered by arguing that this upsurge of concern for workers' rights in the poorer countries is nothing but crass protectionism in disguise. Besides, concern about labour policies in other countries may justifiably be regarded as inappropriately paternalistic and culturally patronizing. The view that finally emerged was that although compliance with core labour standards should legitimately be made a matter for international sanction and concern (just like the violation of basic human rights in South Africa or Serbia), the issue should not be linked to market access or trade policy. The WTO ministerial meeting in Singapore in 1996 declared that it properly falls within the purview of the ILO and suggested that the ILO machinery should be strengthened to deal with it. Earlier, in March 1995, the director-general of the ILO had written to the WTO urging that the members should be required to ratify all conventions prohibiting forced labour or granting workers the right to engage in collective bargaining.

The proponents of globally uniform labour standards tend to forget that higher minimum wages or improvements in standards that raise labour costs may end up doing more harm than good if the consequence is a large drop in employment. There may be other repercussions as well. A ban on import of a particular product produced with child labour may cause the supply of such labour to shift to the production of some non-traded good with worse working conditions and lower wages. Thus trade sanctions impose a welfare cost at home by shutting out cheap imports and have unpredictable and ambiguous impact on the welfare of workers in the exporting country. It is not surprising that economists almost unanimously oppose their use.

Those who defend the rights of the LDCs to maintain their own labour standards sometimes make the mistake of claiming that rights are a luxury good that has no weight in the value system of poor people in developing countries. This is entirely fallacious, as pointed out by Amartya Sen, 'To the extent that there has been any testing of the proposition that the poor Asians do not care about civil or political rights, the evidence is entirely against that claim'.

When workers in advanced countries argue that high labour standards are damaging their competitiveness they should also remember that high standards are a valuable non-cash element in their remuneration. Market logic dictates that if they want to enjoy that benefit and maintain employment at the same time, they will have to accept a cut in the real value of their cash wage either through a wage cut or a currency depreciation. They cannot have it both ways.

The much dreaded 'race to the bottom' also has not been observed in the developed world. The location decision of MNCs is likely to be influenced far more by the productivity of labour and other parameters than the level of labour standards as such. There exists, in fact, evidence to show that low labour standards may actually deter, and not attract, investment by foreign firms. The most important variables remain the traditional ones: infrastructure quality, distance, quality of the labour force, and market size. If anything, it is some LDCs who seem to have suffered from competitive lowering of standards to attract foreign capital. As a group they have become worse off, with no change in relative positions.

GLOBALIZATION AND LOW SKILLED LABOUR

Greater openness to trade and the integration of the world economy at a rapid pace have impacted adversely on the economic condition of unskilled or semiskilled workers everywhere in the world, in advanced as well as developing countries alike. Real wages of such workers have been stagnant or declining in the industrialized countries throughout the 1980s and 1990s. The gap between the earnings of skilled and low skilled occupation groups has been widening as a consequence. Unemployment has also been steadily rising in European countries, concentrated mostly, once again, in the lower end of the skill spectrum. Led by workers' groups, protest against globalization has been on the rise, reaching its peak during the third ministerial meeting of the WTO in Seattle in December 1999. So violent was the agitation that the meeting could not be concluded.

Most of the spectacular growth in world trade during 1950–80 under the auspices of GATT occurred in differentiated manufactured products among structurally similar developed countries. Trade-induced factor dislocation was, therefore, moderate and manageable. The extensive globalization of recent years has changed this radically. Competition from low wage LDCs, both as sources of import and hosts of DFI, has become quite hot. Successful catching up by the NICs and the emergence of China as a vigorous exporter have been significant contributory factors. The demand for the services of unskilled labour has tended to fall sharply in the importing countries. This has been seriously exacerbated by the skill-intensive nature of technological progress in recent years.

Standard trade theory based on factor proportions (Heckscher Ohlin Theory) predicts that opening up of trade will raise the real income of a country's relatively abundant factor. Since the LDCs are better endowed with low skilled labour, greater openness, according to this view, should work in favour of unskilled workers in such economies. But the outcome depends crucially on the ability to export more and that in turn depends on the international competitiveness of a country. As matters stand today, most of the gains from expanded trade with the advanced countries can be expected to be captured by the relatively more efficient LDCs. (Our earlier comments on the likely impact of the MFA phaseout may be recalled.) Thus the market shares of China, Thailand, or Malaysia may rise (and are actually rising) at the expense of India, Pakistan, Bangladesh, Sri Lanka, or Nigeria. Not only is share going down in some major foreign markets, Indian firms are finding it difficult to hold their own even in the domestic market against imports from China or Thailand. This is a case of low skilled Indian workers being outcompeted by their Chinese counterparts in the markets of the USA, the EU, Japan, and India itself. The only effective way of reversing the trend is to raise competitiveness through productivity improvement, quality upgradation, and building up of efficient marketing networks. Indian industry must recover the competitive edge that it has lost through long periods of protection. Exposure to global competition, it is hoped, will force our producers to get rid of the load of accumulated X-inefficiency.

Even when a country is able to export more trade liberalization leads to loss of jobs in the import competing sectors. There will be a time lag before a displaced worker can find another job. Since employment is being created in sectors other than those which are shrinking finding another job is by no means easy. Provision of temporary income support and search and relocation assistance are needed to ease the adjustment problem. Countries like the USA, the UK, France, Canada, and Australia have tended to favour a safety net approach (provision of unemployment insurance), while Sweden, Japan, and Germany have adopted more proactive labour market policies involving assistance for training, retraining, and relocation. Empirical evidence points to the superiority of the latter class of policies in facilitating adjustment. But the design and implementation of such programmes have proved a demanding challenge for governments even in the advanced countries mentioned. Therefore, although the Government of India has decided to set up an assistance programme for workers adversely affected by the forces of liberalization and global integration one should not be too optimistic about its efficacy.

It should be remembered that the standard Heckscher Ohlin prediction depends on a number of special assumptions and may not hold if the analysis is extended to include skill biased technological progress, non-traded goods, or factors other than skilled and un-skilled labour. Even with unchanged technology it may happen that a decline in demand for unskilled labour in the non-traded sector caused by greater openness more than offsets the rise in demand in the export sector. A similar 'perverse' outcome is possible when a third factor is included. Consider a factor T, which is complementary to skilled labour in production. A country has a high ratio of unskilled to skilled labour, but also such an abundant supply of T that it has a comparative advantage in Z, a T-intensive good. Greater openness to trade would raise the output of Z which requires a high ratio of skilled to unskilled labour and could thus drive down the relative wage of unskilled labour. The standard theory finds it difficult to explain the success of unskilled labour surplus India in the field of computer software exports.

Based on the assumption of unchanging technology equally available to all, the Hecksher Ohlin analysis cannot handle technical change biased against unskilled labour. Increased openness in an LDC can be expected to have two effects. Sectoral composition of output may change towards unskilled labour-intensive goods, but at the same time may alter the mode of production against unskilled labour by making domestic producers aware of advanced techniques used abroad and by permitting import of sophisticated capital equip-ment. The net impact may go either way. Also, in the standard analysis based on unchanging production function with constant returns to scale absolute and relative real wages always move in the same direction. If the assumptions are relaxed a fall in relative wage of unskilled labour may go hand in hand with a rise in the absolute level.

Impact of globalization on relative wages also depends on changes in labour market institutions, which enhance or reduce the power of trade unions, affect the level of minimum wages and alter the share of the public sector (where the wage differential is typically narrower than in the private sector). Thus, even as freer trade tends to lower the skilled–unskilled wage gap, decline in minimum wages or other institutional factors may pull in the opposite direction.

Empirical evidence shows that for Hong Kong, Korea, Singapore, and Taiwan the wage gap did indeed narrow during the period of adoption of more outward-oriented policies. Studies have shown that for Malaysia also, even after controlling for the policy of discrimina-tion in favour of indigenous Malays, between 1973 and 1989 there were demand shifts towards less skilled workers due to expansion of export related activities. In Mexico, on the other hand, skill differential in wages widened after the mid-1980s in parallel with extensive trade liberalization. Colombia, Costa Rica, and Uruguay showed a similar trend. Increased openness was also associated with widening differentials in Chile and Argentina in the late 1970s. But in both these cases drastic reduction in the bargaining power of unions under military rule, rather than trade-induced change in relative demand, is possibly a better explanatory factor. Overall, the empirical evidence on this very important issue remains decidedly mixed and inconclusive.

INDIAN AGRICULTURE IN THE NEW ERA

The pre-reform regime in our country was marked by 'urban bias' in the sense that the industrial sector enjoyed a high level of protection through tariffs, quotas, lots of administrative controls, and an over-valued currency, while agriculture was put under export restraint as well as numerous other indirect price controls. Farmers' lobbies, championed by the Shetkari Sangathana of Sharad Joshi, have long vented their discontent and held this bias against agriculture responsible for the perpetuation of rural poverty in India.

These groups enthusiastically welcomed the regime change as the dawn of deliverance and were excited at the prospect of finally obtaining the freedom to sell in foreign markets at prices considerably above the domestic level. There was even talk of growth led by agricultural exports.

As part of pro-trade reforms quantitative restrictions have been lifted on a considerable number of agricultural commodities. For example, there is no more any export control on rice of any variety. Import quotas have been abolished for edible oils, cotton, and sugar. State agencies no longer hold monopolies for import of edible oil and cotton. A considerable number of inputs required by agriculture, aquaculture, pisciculture, horticulture, and animal husbandry have been removed from the negative list of prohibited imports.

While the opening up of trade in foodgrains will boost the income of exporters, the impact on the well-being of the poor is most likely to be negative. Greater exports will exert an upward push on prices and there is a strong positive correlation between poverty and the consumer price index for agricultural labour (CPIAL). Numerous studies have repeatedly confirmed this correlation. So the poorer sections almost certainly stand to lose as a result of any large scale opening up.

The ill effect can be mitigated if export opportunity is kept confined to farm products that do not figure prominently in the consumption basket of the poor. Even then vigilance will have to be there to check diversion of land from food crops to the commercial crops. Otherwise food security may be compromised.

Proponents of liberalization often criticize the above line of reasoning by pointing out that it considers only the cost side but ignores the beneficial impact of export expansion on the income of agricultural labourers. Boost in production will translate into rise in labour demand and, hence, in wages. The rural poor will gain in real terms despite the rise in prices. For this happy outcome to materialize the price elasticity of supply is required to be high so that the production effect can outweigh the price effect. What is the evidence on supply response in Indian agriculture?

Empirical studies show that relative supply of different crops is indeed sensitive to changes in relative price. But the response of overall agricultural output is more strongly influenced by factors such as use of seeds of improved variety and infrastructural factors (such as irrigation, transport, and marketing facilities) than by the price level. Therefore, trade-induced change in relative prices, not backed by improved seeds and adequate infrastructure, can hardly be relied on to impart a sufficiently vigorous and sustained boost to labour demand across the entire rural sector. Public investment in agriculture in India has been languishing over a prolonged period and, thus, acting as a drag on private investment with which it has a complementary relationship. An improvement is possible if the farm lobby can pressurize the government into reversing the trend. For success in export more efficient processing, packaging, and marketing is essential, just as in the case of manufactures. Marketing and processing margins for farm products are currently very high in India by international standards.

There is also the danger that infrastructurally better endowed areas may reap a disproportionately large gain, exacerbating regional inequality. Therefore we advocate a cautious opening up supported by better and more evenly distributed infrastructural facilities. We would also like our farmers to be able to hold their own in foreign markets on the basis of productivity and marketing efficiency, rather than with the help of generous subsidies. Subsidies cannot be altogether eliminated unless all countries do that simultaneously, which is a remote possibility at the moment. But the reliance on subsidies must come down, even if gradually. Without a rise in productivity and marketing skill it will be impossible to face the rising tide of cheap imports not only from the DCs but from other labour-surplus economies (Thailand or China, for example) as well.

A small group of big farmers has so far succeeded spectacularly in hijacking most of the benefits of our agricultural programmes. Export expansion will have little impact on rural poverty and an adverse impact on inequality if small and marginal peasants continue to be excluded from the new opportunities. We conclude by challenging the claim that in pre-reform days agriculture was ruthlessly taxed to subsidize industry. It must not be forgotten that procurements, price controls, and export restrictions were accompanied by huge and ever growing subsidies on credit, fertilizer, electricity, and water. And farmers paid no income tax into the bargain. The argument that agriculture was taxed in the net is by no means beyond dispute.

TRIPS

For the protection of IP several international conventions exist for laying down standards. The major ones are the Paris Convention (1883, revised in 1967, 129 signatories) on patents and trademarks, the Berne Convention (1886, revised in 1971, 111 signatories) on copyright, the Rome Convention (1961, 47 signatories) on neighbouring rights of performers, producers of phonograms, broadcasting organizations, and the Treaty on Intellectual Property in respect of Integrated Circuits (1989, 8 signatories). (It is to be noted that the USA, the EU, and Japan have refused to sign the last treaty, preferring to negotiate reciprocal accords among themselves.) The World Intellectual Property Organization (WIPO) was established in 1967 to administer multilateral IP-related agreements. In 1974 it was granted the status of a specialized agency of the UN. Assisting the developing countries to establish and rationalize their own systems of IP protection has been one of its main activities.

Most net exporters of IP-intensive goods and services were not fully satisfied with the existing conventions which, they felt, dealt inadequately with counterfeiting and other violations of IPR. Since WIPO does not have any effective dispute settlement or enforcement mechanism, they were strongly motivated to put IPR on the GATT agenda because then trade sanctions would be available to enforce agreements.

The USA has long been applying Section 337 of the US Tariff Act of 1930 to impose unilateral sanctions on imports held to be produced in such a way as to contravene IPR that American firms hold under domestic US law. There is no requirement of injury to US producers and the punishment is a ban, rather than an import duty. On numerous occasions tariff concessions extended to Brazil, Mexico, Thailand, Honduras, and South Korea under GSP were withdrawn on the ground of infringement of IPR of American industry. A GATT panel had found Section 337 to be discriminatory in nature. Although the USA refused to change its legislation, the mounting resentment was a compelling reason why it sought to make the general dispute settlement mechanism of WTO available to address IP-related conflicts. To the victims this was preferable to unilateral sanctions by the USA or other OECD countries.

The developing countries, led by India, took the eminently reasonable position that WIPO, not GATT, was the appropriate forum for formulating international rules for IP protection. But, ultimately, the weight of the DCs prevailed and they had to agree to TRIPS in the Uruguay Round. Most of them were trying to move rapidly towards more market-friendly economies with the help of DFI by multinationals. This gave a strong negotiating leverage to the USA and other major exporters of IP. It is easy to twist an arm that is holding a begging bowl. The LDCs, ultimately, had to accept much more than what even the most optimistic representatives of the three big US industries (pharmaceuticals, entertainment, and informatics) had hoped for in 1986 when the preliminary talks began.

The TRIPS Agreement consists of seven parts: (1) a statement of general principles and clarification of the position vis-à-vis the Paris and Berne Conventions, (2) minimum substantive standards with respect to the protection of various forms of IP, (3) obligations with respect to domestic enforcement of IPR, (4) obligations with respect to the facilitation in domestic legal systems of the acquisition and maintenance of IPR, (5) dispute settlement, (6) transitional arrangements, and (7) a WTO-based institutional framework for TRIPS.

Minimum Standards of Protection

With respect to copyrights the basic rules of the Berne Convention are incorporated. Computer software is to be covered as literary work. The conditions governing protection of databases are clearly spelt out. To be eligible, databases should merit the status of 'intellectual creation' by virtue of the selection or arrangement of their contents. The minimum term for copyright protection is fifty years.

The agreement defines the types of marks eligible for protection as trademarks and specifies the minimum rights that must be granted to the owners. Members retain the right to deny registration on grounds that are consistent with the Paris Convention. This Convention permitted denial of registration where the trademark is 'contrary to morality or public order' or 'of such a nature as to deceive the public', or where the use of the mark would constitute unfair competition. A multilateral system of registration of geographical indications for wines and spirits and other commodities is under negotiation. (India could not take advantage of this in the case of 'basmati' rice, because 'basmati' is not a place name.) Protection of industrial designs has been strengthened.

The provisions relating to patents involve the most significant modification of the existing international regime. In accordance with the Paris Convention the patent period will be at least twenty years regardless of the type of innovation, covering both processes and products. This will be a major change for India where, in the pharmaceutical industry, the patent length was only seven years and that only for processes. Permitted exclusions from patentability include 'plants and animals other than micro-organism, and essentially biological processes for the production of plants or animals other than non-biological and microbiological processes'. Breeders' rights are currently regulated by the conventions of the Union for the Protection of Plant Varieties (UPOV). The TRIPS Agreement does not require membership of UPOV.

The Agreement permits compulsory licensing (under which the competent authority grants licence to an applicant who has successfully proved abuse of monopoly power by the patenter) during the patent protection period, provided that the proposed user has applied for explicit authorization on 'reasonable commercial terms' and has been refused. Production under such licensing must be primarily for the domestic market and 'adequate remuneration' must be paid to the patent holder depending on the economic value of the patent. An important issue that remains unresolved is what happens if a member's domestic laws and WTO dispute settlement panels do not concur on the interpretation of 'adequate remuneration' or 'reasonable commercial terms'.

Many developing countries justifiably feel that TRIPS enforcement and dispute settlement rules constitute a massive intrusion into their domestic legal and administrative systems, a degree of control by outsiders that is unprecedented. The Agreement requires that judicial authorities be empowered to issue injunctions, award damages and

BOX 7.3: Major Points of Difference between Indian
Patent Act, 1970, and the TRIPS Agreements

I PA	TRIPS
1. Only process patent in food, medicine, and substances produced by chemical processes for a period of seven years.	Product patent in every field for twenty years for all products.
2. A patent is working only when it is used for production in India. A non-working patent may be revoked.	A patent is working even when not active in local manufacturing. This includes the case where the product is only imported. Non-working patents cannot be automatically revoked.
3. No system exists to protect rights of inventors of plant and seed varieties.	Rights of inventors are to be protected through a system like the Plant Breeders' Act of the USA
4. Compulsory licensing is granted for three years if criteria of public interest such as adequate availability and reasonable price are not satisfied.	Compulsory licensing is permitted under very strict conditions.
5. Onus of proof of infringement is on the patent holder. Infringement proceedings are to be conducted under Indian patent law.	Onus is on the accused to prove he is not guilty of infringement. Protection against infringement is to be ensured by common patent law of all member countries.
6. A ceiling may be imposed on licence fee or royalty that can be charged by the holder.	There is to be no such ceiling.

legal costs to successful right holders and to recommend prompt and effective provisional measures 'where any delay is likely to cause irreparable harm to the right holder'. These requirements, it is feared, will provide powerful levers of control to foreign MNCs.

In 1997 the USA complained that India had violated the provision of Article 70.8 of the TRIPS Agreement which requires that if a developing country wants to delay full application of the Agreement with respect to patents on pharmaceuticals and agricultural chemicals it must make available a means for the filing of patent applications. This will ensure that the rights can be effectively exercised at the end of the transition period. The Government of India had issued certain administrative instructions to the Indian Patent Office. The issue was whether this was sufficient to provide a 'sound legal basis to preserve both the novelty of the inventions and the priority of the applications as to relevant filing and priority dates'. A legislative amendment purporting to establish the required filing system had earlier been subjected to considerable delay in the Indian Parliament. When the panel ruled in favour of the USA, India appealed to the Appellate Body arguing that it should have accorded far more deference to India's own view of its legal system and administrative procedures. The Appellate Body, however, held that under the Agreement the panel had a right to its own interpretation and assessment of a member's domestic law. The verdict was given, just as the panel had done, without seeking any expert opinion on the Indian legal system. This is especially disturbing in light of Article 1.1 of the TRIPS Agreement which declares that 'members shall be free to determine the appropriate method of implementing the provisions of this Agreement within their own legal system and practice'.

Following the establishment of the WTO all members had one year to implement the provisions of TRIPS. The LDCs were entitled to a further period of four years for all provisions with the exception of national treatment (non-discrimination between foreigners and nationals) and MFN. Another five-year delay applies where product patent has to be extended to areas of technology that are currently unprotectable (for example, pharmaceuticals or agricultural chemicals).

There have been some attempts to evaluate the impact of TRIPS on the developing countries. According to one estimate there will be a rent transfer of US$ 8.3 billion per year from the rest of the world to just six DCs, of which US$ 5.8 billion will accrue to the USA alone. Most other studies also point to the conclusion that stronger and wider IP protection will result in a regressive redistribution of wealth from the poorer countries to the richer ones. To be set against this loss is the potential gain from greater access to the markets of the developed world. On another front, better enforcement of IPR is regarded as an essential precondition for a larger inflow of DFI to high-technology sectors. Domestic IP-using industries such as informatics that hope to gain access to cutting-edge technologies through technology transfer tend to favour strong IP protection. If more DFI is indeed desirable, TRIPS, as the necessary price, should be less painful to the LDCs. But, as discussed in Chapter 4, the efficacy of DFI as a cure-all is very much open to doubt.

Moreover, critics have pointed to the experience of South Korea to challenge the claim that stronger IP protection is a must for greater foreign investment or technology transfer. That country was able to achieve technology transfer in numerous activities via licensing and other arrangements during a period in which its IP laws were by no means stronger than those of other countries at a comparable stage of development.

TRIPS and the Price of Medicine

Compared to prices in most countries, developed or less developed, that have product patents, prices of drugs in India (which grants only process patent) are much lower. This is true even at purchasing power parity exchange rates. (Even after necessary adjustments medicine in the USA is almost twenty times costlier compared to India, it is three to four times costlier in Pakistan.) It has indeed been observed that in the global market unbranded generic drugs command gross profit margins that are considerably lower than those for drugs under product patent. So it is to be expected that the TRIPS Agreement will exert a strong upward pressure on the prices of drugs by forcing India to grant patents for processes as well as products from the year 2005.

It has sometimes been argued that since the importance of patented drugs in the Indian market is not high enough it should not matter too much whether product patent is introduced or not. In terms of value of sales, however, the share is not at all negligible. According to a study done in 1993 the combined patent-protected sales value of these products was Rs 328 crore against a total of Rs 3013 crore of the top 500 products. Thus, at a first approximation, about 10 per cent of the value of sales of the top 500 items would be affected by TRIPS in India.

A different and more revealing picture emerges if, instead of the share in the aggregate pharmaceutical market, the importance of patented drugs in several major therapeutic groups is highlighted. The therapeutic segment is the relevant market definition.

The TRIPS Agreement contains some safeguards that can help the patent-offering countries to keep medicine prices under control. The

Table 7.2: Share of Patent-Protected Drugs in India, 1998

Therapeutic group	Share (per cent)
Antibiotics	42
Antibacterials	98
Cardiovascular drugs	51
Anti-inflammatory	21
Antiulcer	99
Tranquillizers	61
Antihistamins	42

Source: Indian Doctors' and Medical Association (IDMA) Bulletin.

most important is the system of compulsory licensing, under which the competent authority can order a licence to be granted on the application of a person who is suffering on account of abuse of monopoly power by a patent holder. As mentioned earlier, establishing 'legitimate reasons' and 'adequate remunerations' is beset with formidable problems and the relentless opposition of large pharmaceutical MNCs make it extremely hard for developing countries to take recourse to compulsory licensing. In Thailand the major anti-AIDS drug is exclusively marketed by Bristol Myers Squibb. The price is beyond the reach of people who earn the minimum wage. The Thai Government wanted to use compulsory licensing to ensure low priced supply to domestic users. It had to abandon the attempt under heavy pressure from the USA which had licensed that particular drug to Bristol Myers Squibb. One representative of the US Patents and Trademarks Office put it like this: 'We acknowledge that our position is more restrictive than the TRIPS Agreement, but we see TRIPS as a minimum standard of protection'. In the meeting on Compulsory Licensing of Essential Medicine held in Geneva in March 1999, Dr Michel Scholtz, Executive Director, Health Technology and Pharmaceuticals, WTO, expressed his concern over the issue because in most developing countries one year's HIV treatment would consume about thirty years' income of the average person. He categorically stated that he respected both patents and TRIPS, but a safeguard is definitely needed to stop overexploitation of private rights and to ensure public health.

Direct price control will be one very effective way of keeping medicine prices down. The Drug Price Control Order (DPCO) that is currently in operation in India has played a crucial role in keeping essential drugs inexpensive and there is nothing in the Uruguay Round agreement that requires the abolition of DPCO. Logical as this agreement is, the trouble lies elsewhere. Once an MNC gets a firm foothold in a country's market, it often succeeds in finding ways of pressurizing the local government into softening direct or indirect price controls. MNCs can use the threat of withholding crucial supplies or even pursuade their home governments to impose trade sanctions against the host countries. In this context a look at the experience of three countries may be instructive.

South Korea changed her patent law in the early 1990s. The share of local companies went down from 54.7 per cent in 1993 to 48.3 per cent in 1997. Price control was kept in operation. MNCs from the EU and the USA started complaining that the price set for their products was too low and that the government was violating the national treatment principle by treating local companies more favourably. Under strong pressure, the South Korean government promised equal treatment and softened price control by allowing a large number of drugs to be imported. Still dissatisfied, the USA threatened that bilateral investment treaties with Korea would be put on hold until all the contentious issues were fully resolved. South Korea was nominated a third tier 'watch country' under Section 301.

Brazil had a soft patent law since the late 1960s, and had performed quite satisfactorily on the pharmaceutical front. It had the largest market among the Latin American countries and registered the highest rate of growth in the late 1990s. Prices of pharmaceuticals were rising at an average annual rate slightly higher than the average rate of inflation. Exports were worth a healthy US$ 120 million in 1996.

Product patents were introduced in May 1997. New investment came in almost immediately from global companies such as Glaxo, Roche, Astra, Hoechst, Smith Kline Beecham, and others. Prices rose by 13 per cent by November, while the general inflation rate was only 4.2 per cent. Allergen raised the prices of thirty-eight products by 20–35 per cent and Alcon increased the prices of twenty-three products by 37 per cent. Together these two companies accounted for 79 per cent of the country's opthalmic pharma market. Between March and July 1999 drug prices shot up by 40–60 per cent. The Brazilian authority set up a committee to investigate 'abusive price escalations'. Asked to justify the price hike, the MNCs put the blame on the devaluation of the currency which had made imports costlier. They vehemently opposed price controls and demanded reduction in import duties.

The government urged doctors to prescribe cheaper domestic substitutes but the appeal did not have much impact owing to the extensive marketing network of the MNCs. A decree on compulsory licensing was passed in October 1999 and elicited the comment from the president of Glaxo Welcome (Brazil) that this might have a serious dampening effect on foreign investment. In August 2001, following the refusal of Roche to reduce the price of anti-AIDS medicine, Brazil announced its historic decision to break the patent law and allow domestic production of the drug. On a previous occasion South Africa also had given permission for importing AIDS medicine at low price.

In Pakistan regulation has always been weak, leaving the pharmaceutical scene relatively clear to the MNCs. Bulk drug production within the country is almost non-existent. Price of about 800 pharmaceuticals were deregulated in 1993 and market prices went up sharply. Transfer pricing is rampant and when the government attempted to encourage parallel imports from Italy and other Asian countries in 1994, the MNCs reacted immediately by withdrawing ninety essential drugs from the market. The same pattern was repeated following the new drug policy proposals of 1995, which tried to impose restrictions on the MNCs. This time the threat was to stop the supply of life saving drugs, curtail R&D in Pakistan, and cut jobs massively. This retaliation succeeded in achieving its objective. The MNCs were given the right to fix their own prices for patented drugs. A 10 per cent cut in prices of forty-six products ordered in February 1999, however, is still in force although the global companies keep complaining and urging further deregulation.

It is sometimes argued by the global companies that they are forced to use large scale transfer pricing and to keep prices high because weak patent regimes in the LDCs cut heavily into their legitimate profits. Thus, transfer pricing and high prices are basically protective devices which can be relaxed if IP protection improves. The flaw in this seemingly plausible argument is that it is credible only if there is a fixed target level of profit for the companies, which is evidently not the case. Transfer pricing and high prices will lose none of their utility in a regime of strengthened monopoly position. What is the harm if high profits can be converted into even higher profits? It will be foolish to suppose that prices will be lowered in a lucrative market with low elasticity of demand just because IP is accorded better protection.

Another argument that has some currency is that a patent bestows upon the innovator 'market exclusivity' rather than monopoly power. The innovator, the argument goes, gets the exclusive right to market the patented product, but not the power to keep substitutes off the market. In the developing countries, however, good substitutes for patented drugs are often not available, an important reason being the practice of the companies to withdraw off-patented products from the market as soon as new patented drugs are introduced.

BOX 7.4: NAFTA and the Pharmaceuticals

NAFTA represents a major victory for MNCs, mostly US-based, in the pharmaceutical industry. Canadian law used to grant patent protection for pharmaceuticals for only ten years and after that there was provision for compulsory licensing. As a result a wide array of inexpensive generic drugs were available in the market entailing substantial cost saving both for the consumers as well as for the government-run programmes for the poor and the elderly. In order to comply with NAFTA and the (anticipated) Uruguay Round Agreement on TRIPS, the law was changed to provide patent protection for twenty years.

Massive, high profile lobbying by the MNCs that stressed the amount of new R&D that would be undertaken in Canada under the new regime, and aggressive unilateral action by the USA, including action under Section 337 of the Tariff Act, succeeded in bringing about a substantial weakening of the Canadian domestic regulatory regime. The present Canadian government, under pressure from activist groups, has initiated moves to reintroduce compulsory licensing of pharmaceuticals on terms consistent with NAFTA.

Source: Trebilcock and Howse (1999).

TRIMS

We have seen in the chapter on MNCs that host country governments often impose conditions like local content requirement on foreign firms operating within their territories. These are frequently accompanied by minimum export performance standards and restrictions on profit repatriation. These policies are collectively known as trade-related investment measures (TRIMS).

Since international trade and international investment are becoming increasingly interdependent and governments are showing intense interest in DFI inflow, it is not surprising that American and European MNCs have spearheaded the attempt to develop an integrated

---

BOX 7.5: Death of an Agreement

The Uruguay Round failed to yield any agreement on a comprehensive set of rules relating to DFI, the TRIMS Agreement being essentially a restatement of the status quo of the 1947 GATT. The DCs attributed this 'failure' to the non-cooperative attitude of the LDCs. The MNCs, however, were not willing to give up so easily on the attempt to achieve a set of comprehensive and binding liberalizing commitments on foreign investment. A set of like-minded nations displaying 'a convergence of attitudes' embarked on a programme to achieve agreement on investment rules that would reconcile the interests of international investors and regulatory states. In May 1995 an OECD Report to ministers was prepared, which proposed the negotiation of a Multilateral Agreement on Investment (MAI) within the OECD forum. Access was open to non-OECD countries provided they were ready to accept its strictures. The central principle of the draft was that governments must not discriminate against or among foreign investors from countries that have signed the agreement—National Treatment and Most Favoured Nation respectively. The rules on performance requirement for foreign investors such as minimum export, domestic content, and domestic sourcing were all prohibited, and so were all technology transfer requirements. Although by May 1997 substantial agreement had been reached on many basic issues including MFN and National Treatment important differences were also surfacing with respect to the relationship of the MAI to environmental and labour standards and cultural policies. Canadian antiglobalization activist groups, who had earlier opposed NAFTA, got hold of a copy of the draft and circulated it on the internet. As accounts of MAI began to appear in the popular press, governments were put on the defensive to justify their negotiating positions to the public at large. It was difficult to refute the charge that the Agreement reflected only the interests of capital because it did not contain any environmental or health or safety exception comparable to that existing even in GATT 1947. The atmosphere of secrecy surrounding the negotiations did not help matters either. In December 1998 MAI negotiations were formally abandoned.

Source: Trebilcock and Howse (1999), Goldsmith and Mander (2001).

framework addressing TRIMS. The list of measures on which they sought disciplines in the Uruguay Round was long. It included local content, export performance and domestic sales requirements, technology transfer and licensing, ownership and remittance limitations, and tax incentives. Most developing countries, on the other hand, put up stiff resistance, arguing that multilateral disciplines on investment-related policies were beyond the scope of GATT.

The TRIMS Agreement that emerged in the Uruguay Round was a compromise. Here, in sharp contrast to TRIPS, the advanced countries failed to achieve what they had originally planned. Basically, the Agreement is little more than an affirmation and moderate strengthening of the GATT 1947 disciplines on national treatment and prohibition of quantitative restrictions on trade flows that directly affect investment policies. All TRIMS inconsistent with GATT are to be eliminated by the developed, developing, and least developed countries within two, five, and seven years respectively. India falls in the second category. (The least developed countries are forty-eight countries of which thirty-two are in Sub-saharan Africa.)

THE DOHA MEETING

After the fourth ministerial conference at Doha in November 2001 the WTO is about to start a fresh round of negotiations on new agendas. During the meeting the LDCs drew attention to more than a hundred 'implementation issues' they wanted to address. The DCs were squarely accused of not delivering on the promises made in the Uruguay Round. Prominent examples include the USA's continuing use of various antidumping duties, the EU's persistence with farm subsidies, and the failure of the rich countries in general to provide adequate assistance to enable the poor countries to comply with the new regulations and build up export capability. They mustered strong opposition to the idea of taking patent on life forms in order to preserve their control over genetic stock vital for agricultural production.

The Ministerial Declaration in Doha does include a commitment for a high-powered committee to review the grievances of the LDCs. The advanced countries have tacitly agreed not to press the labour standards issue too hard in future negotiations. This will work to the advantage of China, which became a member of the WTO in December 2001. The most significant outcome of the conference from the point of view of the developing world is the Declaration on TRIPS Agreement and Public Health. It represents a major victory for Brazil, India, and South Africa which had taken the initiative on this issue. The declaration clearly states that the TRIPS Agreement should not prevent members from taking measures to protect public health and, in particular, to promote access to medicine by all. (The success of Brazil and South Africa in forcing drug companies to back down on the issue of AIDS drugs in 2001 was a big factor behind this victory.) Each member country has the right to grant compulsory licences and the freedom to determine the grounds upon which such licences are to be granted. It has also retained the right to determine what constitutes 'national emergency or circumstances of extreme urgency'. The deadline for patent law compliance by the least developed countries has been extended from 2006 to 2016. This does not represent any gain for major drug producers such as Brazil or India as they do not qualify.

In the area of industrial goods developing countries have complained that peak tariffs in the rich countries remain concentrated on textiles, clothing, leather products, and footwear. The Ministerial Declaration has agreed to negotiate reductions in peak tariffs and tariff escalations that harm the interests of developing countries. It has also opened WTO rules in three areas to future negotiation: (a) antidumping, (b) subsidies and countervailing measures, and (c) regional trading agreements.

On the trade and environment front most LDCs had been totally opposed to bringing environment-related issues into the agenda of negotiations, but the EU insisted on it. The Declaration brings environment into the agenda and calls for negotiations on the relationship between WTO rules and provisions of multilateral environmental agreements (MEA) among members. Trade sanctions by MEA signatories on non-signatories are explicitly ruled out.

In the teeth of very strong opposition by the LDCs, the EU had insisted on inclusion of the so-called 'Singapore issues' relating to multinational agreements on investment, competition policy, trade facilitation, and transparency in government procurement. After a keen tussle the Declaration arrived at a compromise which states that the modalities of negotiation will be decided on the basis of decisions to be taken by explicit consensus in the fifth ministerial conference to be held in Mexico in 2003.

EIGHT

Conclusion

Ideas, knowledge, art, hospitality, travel—these are things which should of their nature be international. But let goods be homespun whenever it is reasonably and conveniently possible; and above all, let finance be primarily national.

John Maynard Keynes

After the demise of the Cold War (Francis Fukuyama's famous 'end of history') the triumph of free market capitalism driven by the neoliberal ideology seemed absolute. For almost a decade nothing could question, let alone seriously challenge, Lee Hsien Loong's arrogance-tinged declaration (quoted in the Introduction). But then, as Europe began to reel under massive and rising unemployment, Japan struggled on to avert negative growth, disaster spread across East Asia, worker demonstrations broke out all over the USA, and crony capitalism revealed its ugly face in Russia, debate on the desirability of unregulated capitalism became possible again. History simply refused to obey Fukuyama.

The advocates of neoliberalism stress the huge opportunities opened up for everybody. 'The rising tide will lift all boats.' They keep warning that failure to grasp the opportunities is the surest way to doom. The poor countries must open their markets, learn to reduce costs, and create a market-friendly environment of law and order and property rights. If they do, they 'emerge'. Poor workers in western economies must learn to upgrade their skills and move out of activities likely to face competition from the low wage countries.

Opponents challenge liberalization and globalization as mere euphemisms for the removal of restrictions on global corporate activity.

Free trade is beneficial, they agree, but only if it is really free and not controlled and manipulated by a handful of multinationals. They point to the rising trend of inequality of income and wealth both within and between national economies of all type, advanced or backward alike. Neoliberalism, according to this view, must be countered, because by tearing down barriers to investment and trade it is providing multinationals unprecedented access to the resources of the earth, pushing the unsustainable, energy-intensive way of life of the industrial countries to all corners of the world.

Several critics have questioned the notion that unprecedented globalization is now going on by pointing out that the developing countries that have gained the most from growing trade and foreign investment have been few, not more than a dozen, although the number is growing. Africa, in particular, has been largely bypassed. In 1999 twelve countries in Asia and Latin America accounted for 75 per cent of total capital flows, while 140 of 166 developing nations accounted for less than 5 per cent. On the outflow side, the bulk of foreign investment is made by a small number of firms from a handful of countries in a narrow range of industries. It is also to be noted that although enhanced factor mobility is taken to be a prominent feature of globalization, there is much less international migration today than during the years before World War I. Harping endlessly on the virtues of freely moving capital and finance, neoliberals stop short of advocating free movement of people. Laissez faire is the slogan of the day, laissez passer (unrestricted travel and migration) seems to be forgotten. Skilled labour has become more mobile internationally, but further development of electronic technology will reduce the need for its movement in future.

Countries with strong governments and at a more advanced stage of social development (with respect to social security health and education, in particular) will be better able to derive benefit from global integration and to withstand its harmful consequences. Through determined public action sustained over decades China has far outstripped all other LDCs in this regard. Most lamentably, our own overall record has been among the poorest in the world. That is why the exposure to global capitalism is so fraught with sinister possibilities for the vast majority of our teeming millions. The Russian economy is in ruins after economic reform (with about 40 per cent of the population hovering around the poverty line, according to one estimate), because the entire government machinery was virtually destroyed under Boris Yeltsin. A strong and committed government, on the other hand, enabled Botswana to benefit from globalization by accepting it on its own terms, and not on terms dictated by the World Bank or the IMF.

Reaction against globalization or the neoliberal ideology in general is steadily gathering momentum. By no means restricted to the ranks of only the unskilled workers, it is resistance to a system that, in the name of efficiency, seeks to destroy regional governments and local culture while handing overwhelming power to faceless corporate bureaucracies in glass-and-steel towers in New York, Tokyo, Geneva, or Brussels. We have already seen how the MAI was unmasked by activist groups in Canada. 10,000 hectares of genetically manipulated cotton (Bollgard Cotton developed by Monsanto) was destroyed on government order in Gujarat. Several organizations have come up all over the world to fight concentration of 'free trade' in the hands of multinationals by promoting fair trade. One of their major objectives is to guarantee better deal for the producers of LDCs and ensure good quality for the consumers. It is maintained, with enough justification, that global poverty is due in considerable part to the manner in which the DCs trade with the LDCs.

The Fair Trade Foundation licenses and promotes the 'fair trade' mark as indicator to consumers that the products are giving a fair deal to the producers in the developing countries. Currently, the products most commonly subject to fair trade marketing are coffee, chocolate, and tea. (Cafédirect is a brand of blended fair trade coffee that is enjoying a rising market share in the UK.) For a period of at least three years producers are paid a guaranteed price above the going market price. There are an estimated 100,000 Mexican farmers growing fair trade coffee by organic methods. Other examples are organic cotton from India, Senegal, Turkey, and Uganda; nuts from Ecuador; fruits from Chile; and bananas from the Caribbean. Spread of fair trade marketing will go a long way towards safeguarding the interests of the rural poor of the world.

In Canada some organizations are promoting symbols that allow consumers to identify food products from their own regions. This is meant to counter type of food system the global firms are trying to promote—one where consumers care only for price and perceived quality. A green-label certification scheme in the Netherlands aims to raise the standard of food production in respect of use of pesticides and chemical fertilizers without forcing local farmers to go for drastic change. Consumers have revealed their willingness to pay premium for better quality. It may be reasonably hoped that, as their economic strength grows, more and more LDCs will come to follow the example set by their more affluent counterparts.

Having deliberated long and hard on the pros and cons of the 'new world order' throughout the book, our message for India is simple: we should definitely try to integrate more with the world since isolation is no longer an option, but the process should be very carefully regulated. The government should get out of non-viable activities in which private enterprise has comparative advantage and concentrate on improving efficiency, transparency, and the building up of social capital (which includes safety nets for the underprivileged).

Select Bibliography

Atkinson, A.B. (1999), *The Economic Consequences of Rolling Back the Welfare State*, MIT Press, Cambridge, MA.

Barro, R. (1996), *Determinants of Economic Growth: A Crosscountry Empirical Study*, National Bureau of Economic Research, USA.

Bhagwati, J. (1997), *Writings on International Economics*, Oxford University Press, Delhi.

Bhattacharya, R.N. (ed.), (2001), *Environmental Economics: Indian Perspective*, Oxford University Press, Delhi.

Buchanan, J., R. Tollison, and G. Tullock (1980), *Toward a Theory of the Rent Seeking Society*, Texas A&M University Press, College Station, Texas.

Cabral, L. (2000), *Introduction to Industrial Organisation*, MIT Press, Cambridge, MA.

Dunning, J. (1993), *Multinational Enterprises and The Global Economy*, Addison Wesley, London.

Ethier, W. (1995), *Modern International Economics*, 3rd edn., Norton and Company, New York.

Falk, R. (1999), *Predatory Globalisation*, Polity Press, London.

Ferguson, P. and G. Ferguson (1994), *Industrial Economics*, 2nd edn., Macmillan, London.

Goldsmith, E. and J. Mander (ed.) (2001), *The Case Against the Global Economy*, Earthscan, London and New York.

Griffiths, A. and S. Wall (1995), *Applied Economics*, 6th edn., Longman, London.

Hoekman, B. and M. Kostecki (1995), *The Political Economy of the Global Trading System*, Oxford University Press, Oxford, UK.

Kenen, P. (2000), *The International Economy*, 4th edn., Cambridge University Press, Cambridge, UK.

Krugman, P. (1998), *The Age of Diminished Expectations*, MIT Press,

Cambridge, MA.

Kumar, N. (1994), *Multinational Enterprises and Industrial Organisation: The Case of India,* Sage Publications, New Delhi.

Naughton, B. (1994), *Growing Out of the Plan in China,* Cambridge University Press, Cambridge, UK.

Parikh, K. (ed.), (1999), *India Development Report, 1999–2000,* Oxford University Press, New Delhi.

Pomfret, R. (1991), *International Trade,* Basil Blackwell, Oxford, UK.

Sachs, J. D., A. Varshney, and N. Bajpai, (1999), *India in the Era of Economic Reforms,* Oxford University Press, New Delhi.

Srinivasan, T. N. (1998), *Developing Countries and the Multilateral Trading System,* Oxford University Press, New Delhi.

Sunstein, C. (1997), *Free Markets and Social Justice.* Oxford University Press, Oxford, UK.

Sutton, J. (1992), *Sunk Costs and Market Structure,* MIT Press, Cambridge, MA.

Trebilcock, M. and R. Howse (1999), *The Regulation of International Trade,* Routledge, London and New York.

Vickers, J. and G. Yarrow (1998), *Privatization: An Economic Analysis,* MIT Press, Cambridge, MA.

Wood, A. (1994), *North-South Trade, Employment and Inequality: Changing Fortunes in a Skill-Driven World,* Clarendon Press, Oxford.

World Bank (1992), *Governance and Development,* Washington, D.C.

World Investment Report (1999), *Foreign Direct Investment and the Challenge of Development,* UNCTAD, New York.

World Investment Report (1997), *Transnational Corporations, Market Structure and Competition Policy,* UNCTAD, Bookwell, New York.

Glossary

Acid Rain

It is mostly produced by sulphur dioxide emissions from industry and volcanic eruptions. Acid rain has already poisoned thousands of Sweden's lakes and left nearly 45 per cent of Switzerland's alpine conifers dead or dying. Depending on wind patterns the acids often fall many hundreds of miles from where the original pollutants were discharged.

Arbitrage

Buying and selling of a commodity or asset in different markets to make profit out of the difference in prices or returns prevailing in the markets.

Bears

These are investors who sell shares in the belief that prices will go down. Bulls buy shares in the expectation that prices will rise in the near future.

Beta Coefficient

The expected percentage change in the value of an asset when the value of the market portfolio of all assets changes by 1 per cent. It depends on the risk of the asset relative to the market and the correlation of its return with market return.

Capital Asset Pricing Model

CAPM postulates a simple linear relationship between the average or expected return on any traded asset and the covariance between the return on that asset and the return on the market portfolio as a whole. The expected return equals the return on a riskless investment plus an excess return proportional to its beta coefficient.

Contract Theory

It attempts to characterize the optimal contract between the principal and the agent within an agency relationship. The best contract strikes a balance between the need to insure the agent (say, the manager of a company) against risk and to give him the right incentives. If the manager is risk-neutral then the best solution will be for him to buy up the firm from the principal (the shareholders) for a fixed fee and keep all the profits for himself. Here both the risk (caused by fluctuation in profits) and the incentive are maximum, but the manager is unaffected by the risk, owing to risk neutrality. At the other extreme is the fixed salary contract which implies minimum risk and minimum incentive. This will be the solution when the manager is extremely risk-averse and goes by safety-first. The theoretical solution for the more interesting intermediate case of risk-averse agent is typically somewhat complicated. The expected (and widely observed) contract of a fixed wage plus a share of profits in some form turns out to be the solution under special assumptions.

Cream Skimming

An entrant snatches a profitable component of the incumbent's business, leaving him with a loss on the rest. It is sometimes used as justification of restrictions on entry, particularly after liberalization.

Cross-subsidy

Nationalized industries often engage in cross-subsidization, using profits from some activities to cover the losses in others. The loss making services are usually those consumed by the poorer sections of the population. For example, in our postal system the price of a postcard is lower than its cost of production while that of an aerogramme is much higher. Cross-subsidy is, thus, an instrument of redistribution, another kind of differential taxation. Advocates of liberalization oppose such practice on the ground that the allocative efficiency of the price mechanism is reduced thereby. One group pays more than the true cost of the service while others pay less. This introduces a distortion in the system. Here is another instance of the equity efficiency tradeoff. So long as poor consumers or backward regions derive genuine benefit from it there is ample reason to continue cross-subsidization even at the cost of some inefficiency. Moreover, cross-subsidization is widely practised by multiproduct firms in the private sector as well.

Debt Crisis

The sharp rise in profits of the OPEC producers after the oil shock of 1973 was followed by a massive rise in resources of commercial banks with which these profits were deposited. The banks soon started lending to the LDCs across the globe (see note on Eurodollar). LDC debt to banks jumped from US$ 15 billion at the end of 1973 to US$ 49 billion only three years later. The situation was sustainable because the borrowers' economies were growing and their export earnings kept ahead of debt service payments. By the beginning of the 1980s, however, the situation had changed radically. The LDCs were hit by the worldwide recession and debt service payments as proportion of exports had climbed up to 24 per cent. Interest rates had risen significantly in international capital markets and many countries had to pay more in interest on their old loans than they could raise by floating new loans.

Unable to meet its obligations, Poland requested creditors to re-schedule its maturing debt in 1981. Soon similar requests were made by Mexico, Argentina, and Brazil. Then in 1983 Mexico suspended payment to banks and started negotiating with the IMF about the policies that had to be followed to qualify for a bail-out. The US government and the Bank for International Settlements moved in to provide the Mexican government with short term credit. This was done to save some big US banks from bankruptcy. When Mexico set forth its commitment to bring down domestic inflation and reduce BoP deficit the IMF authorized a large three-year drawing and per-suaded banks to resume lending, albeit on a smaller scale. Brazil, Argentina, and some OPEC countries such as Nigeria had to pass through a similar process.

Most of the debtors were able to reduce current account deficits, but at the cost of falling standard of living and rising unemployment at home.

Dutch Disease

A boom in primary exports leading to a sharp appreciation of the currency often causes a contraction in the lagging sections by reduc-ing their exports. This happened on a big scale in the Netherlands following a spurt in natural gas exports in the 1970s. The discovery of

North Sea oil had a similar adverse impact on the British and Norwegian manufacturing sectors.

Economy of Scope

This occurs when it is cheaper to produce several products in an integrated process rather than produce them separately. If the cost function $C(q_1, q_2)$ denotes the cost of producing quantities q_1 and q_2, economies of scope are present if $C(q_1, q_2) < C(0, q_2) + C(q_1, 0)$. If this is the case, then merger between two firms will be profitable through a reduction in the cost of production.

Efficient Markets Hypothesis

This is the hypothesis that prices of stocks and securities fully and accurately reflect all information pertinent to forecasting future returns. In its strong form it states that these prices fully reflect all information including both publicly available information as well as information held by insiders. Judging efficiency in practice is very difficult because there is no simple test to check whether prices do in fact reflect all information. An indirect test is to look for unexploited profit opportunities. If some information is not captured in prices someone should be able to beat the market by utilizing that information.

Emerging Economies

These are countries that are in the process of opening up their economic systems on a large scale to grasp opportunities created by globalization.

Eurodollar (Eurocurrency) Market

Eurodollars are those deposited in banks outside the USA. More generally, Eurocurrency deposits are denominated in currencies other than the currency of the country in which the bank is located. Thus Eurofranc deposits are franc deposits held by banks outside France. The bank may even be an affiliate of a French bank.

Banks lending out their Eurocurrency deposits have led to a dramatic internationalization of finance over the past thirty years. Most Eurocurrency loans are made by one bank to another in order to adjust cash positions and net holdings of various currencies. The rate of interest used for these transactions is the London Interbank Offered Rate (LIBOR). The huge current account surpluses of OPEC countries after the first oil shock were placed in the Eurodollar market from which they flowed out to the LDCs in the form of bank loans. Total deposits equalled US$ 315 billion in 1973, in 1984 (beginning of the debt crisis) the value was US$ 2168 billion, and in 1986 it reached the figure US$ 3580 billion.

Two factors contributed to the rapid growth of the market in its first phase. One was political. The Soviet Union, for obvious reasons, did not want to keep its dollar reserves in American banks. It succeeded in finding a French bank to manage its dollar transactions. (The cable address of this bank, EUROBANK, explains the generic name.) The practice soon spread to other countries.

The second factor was the desire to put dollar deposits with non-US banks which were not bound by US regulations, in particular by Regulation Q which placed ceilings on interest rates that US banks could pay depositors. When domestic monetary policy tightened, foreign subsidiaries of US firms switched their deposits from American banks to the Eurobanks. In this way the growth of the Eurocurrency market has substantially undermined the efficacy of financial regulations all over the world.

The market is basically unregulated and its activity is concentrated in Nassau, Panama, the Cayman Islands, Luxembourg, and Bahrain. A big 'Asia-dollar' market is now functioning in Hong Kong and Singapore.

Financial Leverage

This is the use of debt financing to augment the resources of a business unit for a given level of equity provided by owners or shareholders. A company with a high debt-to-equity ratio is said to be highly geared or highly leveraged.

Forward Market

When two parties agree on a transaction they also agree on when that transaction shall actually take place. A spot transaction calls for settlement within usually two business days. But sometimes the agreement is for the transaction to take place further in the future, say, thirty days. Then this is a thirty-day forward contract. Companies involved in foreign trade routinely engage in forward exchange contracts to reduce the risk associated with fluctuating exchange rates.

Futures

A futures contract is an agreement to buy or sell an asset for a given price at a specific date in the future. Unlike forward contracts which are tailor-made, futures are in standardized amounts, mature on standard dates, and are traded over the counter (OTC) or in organized markets such as the New York Mercantile Exchange.

Financial futures are a means of speculating or hedging on interest rates, currencies, or stock prices. Their use has increased exponentially over the past couple of decades. The most important centre is the London International Financial Futures Exchange (LIFFE). The Singapore International Monetary Exchange (SIMEX) allows contracts from one exchange to be traded on another.

An 'option' gives the buyer a right to make a transaction in the future but does not carry the obligation to do so. If one purchases a 'call option' on the dollar, for example, he pays the price of that option now and receives the right to buy a certain number of dollars at a certain price (a strike price) on a specified date (a European call) or at any time until a specified date (an American call) in the future. Buying a 'put option' gives the corresponding right to sell a certain number of dollars.

As the foreign exchange market continues to grow by leaps and bounds after the lifting of capital controls, more and more sophisticated financial instruments continue to be developed. It is now possible to trade in options on futures and in futures on options.

Global Warming

Heightened concentration of heat-absorbing gases, especially carbon-dioxide, is causing a steady rise in the Earth's average temperature. The consequent melting of the ice caps is resulting in rise in sea levels and some of the world's most densely populated coastal areas are facing the prospect of flooding.

Greenhouse Effect

Burning of fossil fuels and destruction of forests increase the level of carbon-dioxide. This and other gases trap part of the heat being reflected from the Earth. Rising temperatures melt snow and ice causing oceans to rise.

Hostile Takeover

This is a change in company ownership opposed by the current management and board of directors. It is usually accomplished by buying up a sufficiently large fraction of the shares from current stockholders to be able to elect a new board (see note on Takeover defence).

Learning Curve (Economy of Experience)

It is a negative relation between unit or average cost of production and cumulatve output since the beginning of production. Cumulative output is a good measure of production experience. Typical industries in which the learning curve is important include shipbuilding, aircrafts, and semiconductors. The empirically observed 80 per cent learning phenomenon suggests that average cost will fall by 20 per cent if the total cumulative production doubles.

The learning curve provides the market leader (who is often the first entrant) with a powerful additional basis for persistent or even increasing dominance. As it sells more cost comes down faster, its competitive position improves, which enables it to sell more leading to further reduction in cost and so on.

Leveraged Buyout (LBO)

This occurs when the stocks of a firm are purchased with funds that are acquired mostly through borrowing that is debt of the firm. As a result the firm becomes highly leveraged.

LIBOR

The London Interbank Offered Rate is the rate at which large banks will lend dollar and other currencies. It is also used by the IMF and the World Bank as a basis for determining the terms of loans to the emerging economies. By offering returns greater than LIBOR on Resurgent India Bonds, the Government of India was able to attract substantial funds from NRIs.

Management Buyout (MBO)

This occurs when a firm is purchased by its managers. MBOs are usually LBOs.

Options

See note on Futures.

Ozone Depletion

The ozone layer (15–18 miles above sea level) acts as a shield against the sun's harmful ultraviolet radiation. Two holes in the layer have been detected—one over the Arctic and the other, the size of the USA, over Antarctica. By 1996, ozone had diminished to around half of its 1970 level, chiefly due to the release in the atmosphere of CFC, chemicals used in refrigerators, packaging, and aerosols.

Pareto Optimality

It is a situation from which it is impossible to improve the welfare of any individual without reducing the welfare of somebody else. Thus there is no slack in the system. The first fundamental theorem of welfare economics states that under certain conditions (of which absence of externalities is the most important) competitive equilibrium achieves Pareto optimality. The second theorem states that under certain conditions (which are more stringent than those for the first theorem) any Pareto optimal state can be attained as a competitive equilibrium.

Perfect Capital Market

This is an ideal situation in which all individuals can borrow or lend at the same rate of interest irrespective of the amounts involved. Lending and borrowing rates will be different when the capital market is imperfect and the terms of contract will typically depend on the volume of transactions and the characteristics of borrowers.

Prisoners' Dilemma

Consider the following payoff matrix where S_1 and S_2 stand for the strategies available to each player. The first entry in each cell is the payoff of player 1.

		Player 2	
		S_1	S_2
Player 1	S_1	a, a	b, c
	S_2	c, b	d, d

Suppose, $c > a > d > b$. If player 1 chooses S_1, player 2 is better off choosing S_2 as $c > a$. If player 1 chooses S_2 instead, even then S_2 remains the best for player 1 as $d > b$. S_2 is the dominant strategy for player 2. Since the situation is perfectly symmetric, S_2 is also the dominant strategy for player 1. So both choose S_2 and the outcome is (d, d), the dominant strategy equilibrium. Both, however, would have gained if each had chosen S_1 because $a > d$. Thus, doing what is individually rational, both end up in a suboptimal situation. This highlights the possibility of conflict between individual self-interest and group welfare.

Revealed Comparative Advantage

It is the most commonly used measure of sectoral competitiveness in trade. RCA for a particular product x for a particular country is defined to be the share of that country's export of x in the total world export of x divided by the share of the country's total exports in total world exports. RCA of unity is the benchmark of 'normal' export performance for product x, while a value exceeding unity is an indicator of competitive strength. It should be noted that being based on realized export values it is not indicative of the export potential of commodities.

SWIFT

A vast number of banks now participate in the Society for World-wide Interbank Financial Telecommunication. Headquartered in Brussels, SWIFT consists of three operating centres that are in turn linked with a network of regional processing centres. Instructions from banks are passed on to the local centre and then the transaction is carried through to its conclusion by SWIFT.

Takeover Defence

Managers have come up with a host of ingenious defences against the threat of hostile takeovers.

Golden parachutes

Incumbent managers cushion themselves against the risk of losing their current jobs by inserting clauses in the remuneration contract providing for very attractive benefits in case a manager leaves after a change of control.

Greenmail

This commonly consists of an offer by the existing management to buy out the shares acquired by the raider at an attractive premium.

Poison pills

These are devices to reduce the value of a company after a change of control. One example is a clause requiring that huge dividends be paid after a takeover. The effect is to raise the cost of acquisition significantly.

Scorched earth policies

These deliberately reduce the value of a firm to make it a less attractive target. One way is to sell off key assets, 'the crown jewels', at throw-away prices.

Staggered or classified board

It is a board in which only a minority of members are up for election in any year, so that the votes of even a majority of shareholders cannot immediately replace a majority of the board.

Supermajority rule

It is the requirement that any change of control must be approved by more than a simple majority of voters. For example, two-thirds or three-fourths majority may be needed.

White knight

This is a merger partner or acquirer deliberately sought out by the target's management to thwart a hostile raider. When Mobil Oil attempted a takeover of Marathon Oil, US Steel played the role of a white knight by coming up with a bid that was accepted by Marathon's management.

Total Factor Productivity

This refers to the part of growth in total output that is not accounted for by growth in use of inputs. On the assumption of competitive markets where factors receive the value of their marginal products, growth in TFP is calculated by subtracting from growth of output the weighted sum of growth rates of inputs. The weights are the income shares of the respective inputs.

Venture Capital (Risk Capital)

This is a loan or equity capital supplied to entrepreneurs who are offering or trying to develop new and innovative products and processes. Finance from conventional sources is not available due to the high risk involved. The rate of interest is usually high and an element of ownership passes to the investors who take an active part in the management of the projects.

Index